THE POWER
OF YOUR FAITH

Dr. Eula Payne-Williams

iUniverse, Inc.
Bloomington

THE POWER OF YOUR FAITH

iUniverse books may be ordered through booksellers or by contacting:

iUniverse
1663 Liberty Drive
Bloomington, IN 47403
www.iuniverse.com
1-800-Authors (1-800-288-4677)

Because of the dynamic nature of the Internet, any web addresses or links contained in this book may have changed since publication and may no longer be valid. The views expressed in this work are solely those of the author and do not necessarily reflect the views of the publisher, and the publisher hereby disclaims any responsibility for them.

Unless otherwise noted, all Scripture quotations are from the Scofield Study Bible, King James Version. Copyright 1909, 1917, 1937, 1945 by Oxford University Press, Inc., New York, New York.

Any people depicted in stock imagery provided by Thinkstock are models, and such images are being used for illustrative purposes only.

Certain stock imagery © Thinkstock.

ISBN: 978-1-4759-6411-0 (sc)
ISBN: 978-1-4759-6412-7 (e)

Printed in the United States of America

iUniverse rev. date: 12/04/2012

In memory, of my dear friend, brother, and mentor,
Brother Albert Bailey "Skeeter" Jones.
Thank you for your love, support, and concern. You were
always there to encourage and promote and to cheer me on.
You let me know that with God all things are possible.
I love you and I will miss you, my friend.
Rest in peace!
Until then …

Table of Contents

Preface

Entering the house from my Sunday morning worship service, I proceeded to change into something more comfortable. Then I fixed a bite to eat and sighed deeply. Oh my, it was good to be able to come home, close the door, and shut the world out for a few moments.

As I stretched out on my couch, something caught my eye on the television: instructions on breast self-examination. I nonchalantly raised my arms above my head and examined my breast as she instructed. I thought I felt a knot. Immediately I sat up on the couch and then consoled myself by saying, "That was nothing; I don't know what I'm doing anyway." For some reason, periodically throughout the evening my hand would somehow find its way to my breast. So the next day I called my doctor for an appointment—just to be sure. Of course I told myself, "It's nothing; but it's better to be safe than sorry."

After my doctor's examination, she ordered X-rays and I waited, trying to read magazines. I was hoping it really was "nothing," but all the time I wondered why one breast had a knot and the other did not. Finally, the doctor returned and told me that, yes, there was a lump in my breast. She was referring me to a specialist. When I met with the specialist, he informed me that a biopsy was necessary, and then he proceeded to give me a date for the procedure. I told him that I needed to attend my church council and asked for a date after I returned. It was granted.

In the days following, I fasted and prayed continuously and made my request known to the body of believers. I arrived at the council and when I checked the program, I noticed that the women's department was having early morning prayer. I made it my business to attend.

Entering the sanctuary, I knelt before the Lord. Everyone was very quiet. I asked the presider if it would be all right for me to walk with my arms up, praising the Lord during this time, and she said that would be good. As I walked, praising the Lord and praying for others, I became engrossed in what I was doing. The anointing filled the temple and oh, what a mighty feeling it was!

After prayer, I returned to my hotel to prepare for the daily service, but in preparation for my shower I noticed blood and pus in my bra. I was flabbergasted. "What is that?!" The Lord said to me, *While you were praising Me, I was healing you.*

Returning home, I went for my appointment for the biopsy. The doctor stated he wanted to do another X-ray before the procedure. When they had taken the X-ray, I sat in his office waiting for him to return. The doctor entered the room, looking at me in disbelief. "It's gone; there is nothing there," he stated. "What happened?" I described the encounter with the anointing in the council service. He looked at me and said, "It was there, because the skin in that area is different from the rest. You can tell something was there, but now it's gone. Therefore I'm giving you some cream to put on the tough part of the skin, and in a few days it will be like the rest of the body."

I told the doctor, "God is a healer." He looked at me with that subtle smile. "I know!"

As you read this book, it is my profound prayer that *your faith* too will be increased!

Dr. Eula Payne-Williams

Acknowledgments

My deepest appreciation to my husband, Bishop John Williams, a man of wisdom and understanding. Thanks, Love, for your patience and support during the writing of this book. You have always been here for me, and I'm eternally grateful. I love you!

Special thanks to my church family at El Bethel Kingdom Church for their love, support, and prayers. And especially for my spiritual daughters, Arlene Mayo and Lori Chaney, who kept telling me, "Mom, you can do it!"

Most important, my sincere gratitude to my Lord and Savior, Jesus Christ, for His great love wherewith He has loved me, and the Holy Spirit who has inspired and guided me through this yet another project. *Thank You, Lord!*

Introduction

The purpose of this writing is to share and strengthen the faith of God's people. The adversary has launched his attack at the patience of the people of God, but faith is the bondage breaker! *Faith* is a powerful force which is proven by the Lord's declaration that it's able to move mountains. *Faith* laughs and triumphs over impossibilities. *Faith* does not believe that God can; it knows that He will. For the writer of Hebrews lets us know, by faith, the warriors of the early church subdued kingdoms. The apostle John also encourages us to believe that faith can overcome the world (1 John 5:4).

It is fitting to consider faith after repentance, seeing that true repentance merges into faith as the blossom ripens into fruit. Tears of sincere grief over sin lead to a saving trust in God. Without faith, repentance recedes into indifference or moves into hopeless remorse. Faith is vital in that it leads the repentant soul to God, first to receive His forgiveness and then to appropriate His resources for daily victory, holiness, and inspiration for effective service.

The importance of faith is indicated by the fact that all men are dependent upon it as the avenue of access to God. Sinners, convicted of their need, must exercise faith in God as one ready to pardon them, if they are to be saved. Saints, saved by grace through faith in Christ, must continue to believe. For the Scriptures state, "As ye have therefore received Christ Jesus the Lord, so walk ye in him" (Colossians 2:6). Hopefully, your faith will be enhanced by the testimonies of the various individuals and with the information of this document.

Since the days of becoming a Christian, many things have changed. For example music, dress, decor, activities that we can participate in, leadership, and others. When you see the drastic change, it causes one to question, *How long, oh Lord?* But the age-old reply returns: "For yet a little while, and he that shall come, will come, and will not tarry" (Hebrews 10:37).

Preparation is not an option, but it's *essential*! For the Lord stated to His disciples, "…Nevertheless when the Son of man cometh , shall he find faith on the earth" (St. Luke 18:8). The love of many has waxed cold, therefore leaving the people of God callous, aloof, and indifferent. *Faith* has always been the main ingredient for pleasing God and for developing a people for His namesake.

Faith is one of the greatest qualities of a Christian's life. It is the foundation of the inner man that enables the building of hope, love, peace, and all other attributes of a life that is ordered by the will of God. Faith gives hope, meaning, and purpose to all knowledge. It is fundamental to our relationship with God. The only spiritual ingredient that supersedes faith is charity: "And now abideth faith, hope, charity, these three; but the greatest of these is charity" (1 Corinthians 13:13).

I pray that you will gain power from this book. Its goal is to strengthen, inspire, and exhilarate. The enemy has devised a plan to attack the faith of Christians, but we must always keep in mind that "No weapon that is formed against you shall prosper; and every tongue that shall rise against thee in judgment thou shalt condemn" (Isaiah 54:17). For it is the power of *your* faith that will carry you through!

Chapter 1
What Is Faith?

"You didn't have enough faith," Jesus told them. "I assure you, even if you had faith as small as a mustard seed you could say to this mountain, 'Move from here to there,' and it would move. Nothing would be impossible."

(Matthew 17:20 NLT)

I think the whole concept of faith is one of the most misunderstood ideas that we have—misunderstood not only by the world but by the church itself. The very basis for our redemption, the way in which we are justified by God, is through faith. The Bible is constantly talking to us about faith, and if we misunderstand that, we're in deep trouble.

The Protestant Reformers recognized that biblical faith has three essential aspects: *notitia*, *assensus*, and *fiducia*.

Notitia refers to the content of faith, or those things that we believe. We place our faith in something, or more appropriately, someone. In order to believe, we must know something about that someone, who is the Lord Jesus Christ.

Assensus is our conviction that the content of our faith is true. You can know about the Christian faith and yet believe that it is not true. Genuine faith says that the content—the *notitia* taught by Holy Scripture—is true.

Fiducia refers to personal trust and reliance. Knowing and believing the content of the Christian faith is not enough, for even demons can do that (James 2:19). Faith is only effectual if, knowing about and assenting to the claims of Jesus, one personally trusts in Him alone for salvation.

Now, what really is faith? Faith, in fact, is something that you and I exercise every day in our lives. And we've exercised it from the very moment we were born. I suppose it's true that our mother even encouraged us to feel that we could trust her when we lay in her arms. And we learned day by day that was true—she would not drop us, she was reliable, and we could put our faith in her arms.

So as we grew up and came to the age of two or three or four years old and our mom would ask us to jump from one chair into her arms, we would jump because we felt that we could put our faith in her because she had never let us fall before. And every time we observed her, every time we experienced the stability and the safety of her arms, we were not disappointed, and so we learned to put our faith in her.

It was the same when we began to ride on a bicycle. We started to find out that the bicycle would carry our weight. Then as we were taught how to balance, we found that it was possible, amazing though it was, to push the bicycle along on the ground in such a way that we could stay up even though it had only two wheels. And we began to put our faith in the bicycle and in our ability to ride it and to stay up all the time.

And so in all of our lives, we have gradually come to put our faith in all kinds of things. If I ask you, "Would you put your faith in that chair that is sitting opposite you in your office or in your home?", you would probably reply to me, "That chair? Yes, yes I would put my faith in that chair. That is, I would gladly go over and sit on that chair, because I have observed it holding other people. It has held me on many occasions, and I'm prepared to bet my life on the strength of that chair."

It is the same in all kinds of more important and vital matters. In connection with your bank account, you have absolute faith that when you write a check and send it to a certain person, your bank will forward to them the necessary amount of money as long as it's in your account. You put faith in your bank to do that.

So it is of course every time we step into a plane. We put faith in the incredible theory of aerodynamics that assures us that the mass of metal is going to lift into the air and be able to cross thousands of miles of ocean. Then it lands us safely in another country, even though to our ordinary eyes and our ordinary intellect, we cannot understand why that plane could possibly rise off the ground like that. And yet we put our faith in it because we've seen it happen again and again.

This goes on throughout all of our life. We'll often allow ourselves to be sedated by some stranger in a hospital because we have absolute faith in what the hospital has done with other people. We have even seen other hospitals do this with our own relatives, and we have seen doctors and surgeons perform surgery. We'll put our faith in a great many unknown people and unknown events and unknown techniques, simply because we have observed things in the past and we have good grounds for putting our faith in those things.

So practically every day in our life, we exercise faith a thousand times. We breathe because we put our faith in the fact that the air is clean enough to breathe and is not filled with poisonous gas. In all kinds of manifold situations, we put our faith again and again in people, in things, in events, in techniques, in strategies, in processes that actually on many occasions we have not tried before, but we have observed other people trying them. So when we think of faith, let's not think of something strange and superstitious; let's not think of something religious or something irrational. Let's see that faith is something that we practice every day in our lives.

Faith is the confident belief or trust in the truth or trustworthiness of a person, idea, or thing. The Greek word used in these New Testament Scriptures is *pistis*, which is from the word *patho*, a verb or action word meaning "to believe, persuade, have confidence in, be confident." We know that the Bible describes faith as "the substance of things hoped for, the evidence of things not seen" (Hebrews 11:1). By describing faith as a substance though, we consider it to be something that exists only in our mind or spirit. The Word of God is telling us that it is of substance—faith is real. It is from the word *hypostasis*, which means it is the foundation for what you believe. It is put up under what you believe, like the floor you are standing on—it is not imaginary, but has actual existence!

And Jesus said unto them, Because of your unbelief: for verily I say unto you, if ye have faith as a grain of mustard seed, ye shall say unto this mountain, Remove hence to yonder place; and it shall remove; and nothing shall be impossible unto you.

(Matthew 17:20)

Consider the size of a mustard seed when you compare it to the size of a mountain. Next to a mountain, the mustard seed would not likely even be visible, because the magnitude of the mountain would overshadow it. But what Jesus is conveying here is that the size of the mountain is not the obstacle! It cannot withstand faith! Faith is so potent, it is so full of strength, that a teeny tiny bit of faith is strong enough to move an object the size of a mountain! It is described as being so tiny by the Lord, yet so full of dynamic power, that the size of the mountain is not even of consequence! God hasn't called you to say something prophetically that cannot happen, but rather, He has called you to know the power you are working with! He has called you to know that nothing, no matter how sizeable it may appear to be, can hinder you doing the will and work of God!

The key of Faith. When a man hath liberty to go into the treasure-house of a king, to enrich himself, he will first seek the keys wherewith to open the doors; so, if we desire to be enriched with God's grace, we must first labor to have faith, which is the only key of God's treasure-house, and secures us all graces needful both body and soul.

—Cawdray

Prayer is the key and faith unlocks the door.

And the Lord appeared to Solomon by night, and said unto him, I have heard thy prayer, and have chosen this place to myself for an house of sacrifice. If I shut up heaven that there be no rain, or if I command the locusts to devour the land, or if I send pestilence among my people; if my people, which are called by my name, shall humble themselves and pray, and seek my face, and turn from their wicked ways; then will I hear from heaven, and I will forgive their sin, and will heal their land. Now mine eyes shall be open, and my ears attend unto the prayer that is made in this place. For now have I chosen and sanctified this house, that my name may be there forever; and mine eyes and mine heart shall be there perpetually. And as for thee, if thou wilt walk before me, as David thy father walked, and do according to all that I have commanded thee, and wilt observe my statures and my judgments; then will I stablish the throne of thy kingdom, according as I have covenanted with David thy father, saying, There shall not fail thee a man to be ruler in Israel.

(2 Chronicles 7:12–18)

How often do we look for immediate answers to our prayers and when nothing happens, wonder if God has heard us? God does hear, and He will provide for us, but we must trust that He will answer at the proper time.

In Second Chronicle 7:14, Solomon asked God to make provisions for the people when they sinned. God answered with four conditions for forgiveness: (1) humble yourself by admitting your sins, (2) pray to God asking for forgiveness, (3) seek God continually, and (4) turn from sinful behavior. True repentance is more than talk—it is changed behavior. Whether we sin individually, as a group, or as a nation, following these steps will lead to forgiveness. God will answer our earnest prayers.

Prayer is defined as speaking or communicating with God. For a person to pray there must be (1) an acknowledgment of God's existence, (2) hope that God knows and cares about us, and (3) expectation that God is able and willing to respond to us. Prayer as described in Scripture is an expression of covenant relationship. According to the Old Testament, God established a special relationship with Abraham and his descendants. According to the New Testament, God in Christ, reached out beyond Israel to establish a personal bond with all who would accept His offer of salvation.

Faith is belief, confidence, trust, and reliance. In the Bible, religious faith is a life-shaping attitude toward God. The person with faith considers God's revelation of Himself and of truth to be certain and sure. The person with faith then responds to God with trust, love, and obedience. God made promises to Abraham, and the Bible says, "Abraham believed the Lord, and God credited to him as righteousness" (Genesis 15:6).

To be *righteous* means to be rightly clothed. That is what we are when, like Abram, we simply take God at His word. Righteousness: God thought it. Jesus bought it. The Spirit taught it. Satan fought it. But children of God, we got it! We are robed in righteousness.

Why do you think the Lord made His Word so simple to understand? Does God desire to confuse His children? Of course not! He wants us to put all of our hope and trust in Him even when it looks utterly impossible to men. This brings God the most glory.

Will we have the faith to believe that God's love is greater than we ever imagined, and that He is bigger than we ever thought possible? Will we believe that "With men this is impossible; but with God all things are possible"(St. Matthew 19:26). Faith is the key "and without faith, it is impossible to please Him" (Hebrews 11:6).

Faith is obedience:

> Now the Lord had said unto Abram, Get thee out of thy country, and from thy kindred, and from thy father's house, unto a land that I will shew thee: And I will make of thee a great nation, and I will bless thee, and make thy name great; and thou shalt be a blessing. So Abram departed, as the Lord had spoken unto him; and Lot went with him: and Abram was seventy and five years old when he departed out of Haran.
>
> (Genesis 12:1–2, 4)

Faith is to obey God. God told Abraham to go to a land that He would show him, and Abraham obeyed God by moving at God's command. His faith was based on what God said. If he had gone by what he could see and what his physical senses told him, he never would have received God's promise. His obedience earned him the title of "the father of faith." Abraham believed according to what God said, not according to how he felt. He didn't believe his feelings; he didn't believe based on what he saw; he didn't believe his physical senses. His faith was based on God's promise. God told him to move and he moved. Faith is obedience; it's not based on what you see; it's what you don't see, because if you could see it you wouldn't need faith.

There is no need to wish for a loaf of bread if you have five dollars in your possession; simply go to the store and purchase the bread. But you need faith when you are hungry and you don't have money to purchase the bread.

I recall while on the mission field, we had no food to eat. The Spirit informed me to set the table for dinner. Of course I was a little hesitant. I was thinking, *Why set the table if I don't have food?* but I obeyed. I set the table completely with plates, glasses, silverware, napkins—the whole nine yards. Just as I was placing the last fork on the table, there was a knock at the door. Evangelist Foster answered the door. Someone had been grocery shopping for us and was there to deliver the groceries. Faith is obedience—when God speaks, move!

Here is another time when God spoke. Growing up in church and not being allowed to participate in any outside activities, councils and conventions were really the only things that we had to look forward to. Therefore, when it was council time, we were ready to go. This particular time, I wanted to attend the council but had no money. As I sat thinking what to do, the Lord spoke to me and said, *Get up, pack your suitcase, and set it beside the front door.* I responded, and when the luggage was packed and setting by the front door, the phone rang. I answered it and the voice on the other end (Pastor Wilma Lloyd) asked what I was doing and if I could come to her house (about a two-minute walk). I responded by saying yes. When I reached her home, she informed me that the Lord told her to give me this, and she placed money into my hands—enough for my trip to the council. God spoke and I obeyed.

Faith is obedience. The beautiful reply of a child when asked "What is faith?" was "Doing God's will, and asking no questions." Faith seems not quite natural to the modern mind. The mind is rational, while faith is irrational. The mind is logical; faith is illogical. The mind is also doubtful, while faith is doubt free. In our modern culture, we have become more dedicated to doubt than to unbridled possibility. We are more committed to the calculations of the rational mind than to the holistic wisdom of the spirit. When we put more stock in the workings of our rational mind than on discerning a deeper truth beyond the intellect, faith seems relegated to a precariously irrelevant position.

However, in a very real sense, faith is the only way out of human limitation. Why? Because lack of faith is a negative story of the mind. X is possible, but Y is not possible. This will work, but that will not work. I am suffering today, so I will suffer tomorrow. Faith is the decision to step out of ego and deny its claim on a finite reality. Faith is about possibility. It is utter positivity.

An unknown sage once said, "God does not ask about our ability, but our availability." Are we available to believe in something higher than our own ego-mind? Are we available to trust in a pervading wisdom that can know and do everything? Are we available to suspend doubt and disbelief and live in utter positivity?

It is my consensus with Robert Schuller when he stated, "I would rather err on the side of faith than on the side of doubt."

Chapter 2
If You Believe, It Will Happen!

Faith is a bird that feels dawn breaking and sings while
it is still dark.

—Rabindranath Tagore

"Madam, do you mean to tell me that you expect to buy a brand-new car, with no money down?"

The salesman stared at me from across his desk, with his tailored suit and freshly ironed shirt and that all-over-your face smile when I first came in. He had shown me all the cars on the showroom floor, and I didn't see anything there that I wanted. Then he proceeded to take me downstairs where there must have been at least two hundred new cars.

I looked over to the far left, and there I saw the beauty that I would look so good in. It was so brand-new: burgundy top and interior and white body; with only three miles on it. After touching it, and rubbing lightly as if it would break, and examining the inside, in my mind I could hear all the "ahs" and "oouch" and "girl, that's a bad car!" I could just see myself driving down the highway and hoping to see some of those same people who had sneered at me when I drove my old hooptie with the smoke coming out of the back as I drove off from a light at an intersection.

When I drove and I could see that a light was red, I would slow down gradually and pray that the light would change to green by the time I got to it. I did not want to put my foot on the brake and come to a complete stop for fear the car would stop completely if it didn't keep moving. And as the light changed to green and once again I didn't have to stop, I would press the accelerator. With that press, smoke would come from the back and everyone in back of me would be under a great cloud (not a great cloud of witnesses as in Acts, but a great cloud of smoke). Drivers would pull from behind me, and I could hear their looks as they came even with me, looking over with disgust and saying, "You need to trash that piece of junk." Yes, I do hope I will see them again while I'm driving in my new beauty.

"Ms. Payne," the salesman said, bringing me back to reality, "do you like this one?"

"I love it; this is the one I'm going to get."

"Also Ms. Payne, with this car you don't have to worry about having a flat tire." (Then he went on explaining something about the tires that I didn't understand then and don't understand now.) "Therefore, you don't have to worry about changing a tire or being caught out by yourself and getting a flat."

I didn't know what kind of tires were on it, but with that remark he definitely was looking at his commission for that day—at least that's what he thought.

I like to reminisce about how I got there and what the Lord had spoken to me prior to arriving. Sitting at my desk in my office, I said to the Lord, "I need a car." He in turn said to me, *Well, go and get it.* I had no money (which meant no down payment), and only the old car initially described (for which I would have given you fifty dollars just to get rid of it for me). "Faith without works is dead" (James 2:20). With a surge of energy, excitement, and anticipation, I informed my boss that I had an appointment downtown and would need a few more minutes for lunch. He told me to take as much time as I needed.

Hooptie and I (well not quite a hooptie, but close) got into the mainstream of travel and proceeded downtown to the dealership. As I entered the door with my suit and heels, dressed like the executive that I was, I just needed a car. The salesman approached me, smiling from ear to ear with, "Good afternoon, may I help you?" I responded with, "Yes, I'm looking for a car."

Finding what I wanted, we returned to his office to do the paperwork. He finished recording all of the information, and now we were at the line that said "down payment." He asked how much I wanted to put down. I looked straight into his eyes and said, "Sir, I don't have any money for a down payment." He looked as if he had seen an ignorant ghost.

"You mean to tell me, you want a new car with no down payment?" Our eyes were fixed on each other. He asked how I planned to buy a new car without a down payment. Without dropping my head and continuing to look him in his eyes, and with the boldness and assurance of anyone with a down payment, I said, "The Lord sent me."

He froze in time for a few seconds as if he were undergoing an out-of-body experience and someone was talking to him privately. He finally returned mentally to the room with me and said, "If the Lord sent you, I better continue to write." Let us remember: faith is that knowledge in our hearts that's beyond the reach of proof.

"Are you driving a car now?" he asked. And we went out to see it. He asked, "Can you get me twenty-five dollars cash," and of course, I had that. He looked at the car and kind of shook his head, and he smiled and I laughed. Back inside, still a gentleman and treating me like a lady, on the down payment line he wrote $1,600. And that day, I drove a brand-new car off the showroom floor because I believed God was going to do it for me.

When he looked at me, the enemy wanted intimidation to take over, but I refused to drop my head—you see, faith does not hesitate at what it wants. Name faith and hold to it until it's brought to fruition. Faith takes the attitude of "Lord, if You don't come today; I'll be right here waiting on You tomorrow; and if You don't show up tomorrow, I'll be waiting on You the next day—however long it takes, because, I'm depending on You and You alone. I will stay here until You show up. I will not doubt You; I will trust You because You promised to deliver me, and a promise is a promise!" Faith is reacting positively to a negative situation.

I was quite impressed and encouraged by the testimony of an evangelist while in London, England, and it blessed my soul. It is my desire that it will increase your faith also.

> "And whatsoever ye shall ask in my Name, that will I do, that the Father may be glorified in the Son. If ye shall ask anything in my Name, I will do it"
> (John 14:14).

I remember it all very clearly. We were on our way back from vacation in Ft. Wayne, Indiana. We had gone to see my husband's family and friends. It had been a great weekend. Before we had left, I hadn't taken care of household chores, which meant there were no groceries in the house. So I decided after church the next day (since it was going to be so late when we got back) I would just go get some cash from the ATM and just pick up something for dinner.

Well after church I did just that. After leaving the bank machine, I looked at the receipt to record in my register the transaction and correct balance, and to my surprise the amount was not matching what I had figured. Now, before we left for vacation we deposited my paycheck and took the trip using Darrell's, so there should have been about $600 in the account, but the receipt showed $4,500.

Immediately I became excited and nervous at the same time … what was going on? I shared all this with Darrell, and we decided on his way to work tomorrow he would do another inquiry at the bank, and we would go from there. After doing so, the balance was still the same. We called the bank and said, … "We have $4,000 in our account that we did not put there. Could you check this for us?" "Sir, we have checked and everything is in order. It appears there was a deposit on last Monday and another for today. Your correct balance is $9,000."

Well, by this time we had no clue what to do next, so we decided to just spend what we knew we put in the account and to talk to our pastor. After speaking to him, he assured us that as God delivered the children of Israel and brought them into the Promised Land, so had He delivered us … reminding us they had to fight once they were there. Well, for the next few weeks we continued to get deposits in our account, bringing our balance to over $25,000! By this time, my husband had reminded me, ... "What have you been praying for?"... I had been asking God to help us get debt free. ... *Wow.* I had been so shocked by what was going on, I had forgotten what I had been asking for. And true to His word He did it.

You are probably wondering how this happened. Well my husband calls it the blessing that touched no man's hands. ... What brought it to a close was when we received a corrected deposit slip from the bank stating the corrected deposit amount that was in our favor. When I turned over the deposit slip, it had the name of a particular church in the city with our address and account number. We had banked with this bank for five years and never had a problem. I immediately called the pastor of the church, told him all that had happened, and asked him to check their account. He got back with me later that day saying all was in order with them. ... "Thank God for your blessing." After notifying the bank, we had to secure an attorney; of course they were now accusing us of breaking the law even though we had documented calls all along of what was going on, and they assured us that "it's in your account, it is your money."

To get to how God did it ... somehow the printing company put our account number on this church's deposit slips (only one package); every time they deposited into their account, it duplicated into ours! Every Monday when they went to the bank, we received in our account what they deposited. The attorneys and bank were so amazed at how this could have happened; they wrote it off as an error and asked us to sign a paper stating we would not disclose the name of the bank.

The financial blessing that touched no man's hands, and all I did was ask in His Name and believe! This is powerful—compelling!

I'm yet praising God for my healing from a terrible car accident. I was driving from California to Mississippi for a national convention. In the desert of Arizona, driving at the speed of seventy-five miles per hour, we had a blowout. The car overturned three times, and each time it crushed the head of the driver. The mortician told us that she could not have lived, because every bone in her head was crushed.

The noise from the paramedics and the helicopters flying over our heads, along with other noise, was almost unbearable. I could hear people talking and finally moving toward me to put me on a stretcher before lifting me to the helicopter. Once again, I heard someone say, "She is dead." As they situated me in the helicopter, preparing me for my first helicopter ride, I heard the paramedic say, "Stay with me. You are going to be all right. Tell me; what's your name?" I assumed they were trying to keep me talking so that I would not lose consciousness. As they continued flying, I tried to talk, but couldn't get the words to come out of my mouth. I thought I was talking, but apparently I wasn't, because I could hear the paramedic say, "That's okay; it's going to be all right." Thank God for the men and women who have dedicated their lives to serve the injured. Those two young men were very comforting and continued to reassure me that I would be fine. Their words helped me hold on to life and continue to fight!

After a short distance, the helicopter began to fly lower, and as it landed, I could hear voices. The hospital staff was waiting on the arrival of the helicopter. They rushed over, put me on a stretcher, whisked me into a room, and began cutting off my clothes. They worked on me seemingly for hours. I didn't remember very much, other than being stuck a few times with a needle. I recalled waking up in a room and trying to look around, but being unable to move. I did remember that I and the deacon's wife were in the same room; she too had to be flown to the hospital, but in a different helicopter. We had both made it out alive, thanks be unto God. As I lay there, I wished that I could talk to my mother, but she was about two thousand miles away. However, I remembered feeling the presence of the Lord, and just knowing that He was there, I knew that I would be all right. He had promised me that He would never leave or forsake me, and if I ever needed Him, I really needed Him now.

After all the examinations and settling me down into a room, the doctor came to deliver the news to me. "Paralyzed from the waist down" was the diagnosis he gave me when he entered my room and looked down on me with pain in his eyes. I was hurt, disappointed, and disillusioned. What would a twenty-five-year-old girl do in a wheelchair for the rest of her life? All of my dreams had gone up in smoke.

I cried and cried until there were no more tears. At last I went to sleep, only to be awakened by what I thought was a light. I began stirring, trying to wake up, and finally I was able to remember where I was and what had caused me to be there. Oh yes, I was in the hospital because there had been an automobile accident.

There was something strange going on; was that light moving? No, of course not; that was silly! It was just the reflection from the light in the hallway. Since the door was slightly ajar, it could have very well been coming from the hall. I stared in shock and exclaimed, "Oh, my God, that light is moving. That is not the reflection from the light in the hallway!" As my eyes were fixed on this light, it moved into my room and stood at the foot of my bed. It stopped for just a moment, and very slowly it moved to the right of my bed until I could no longer see it.

I couldn't follow the light because of the instruments and IVs connected to me, so I laid there trying to process what had happened. Suddenly, I felt as if someone had poured a cup of warm water down my back, and as I gasped for air from the shock of it all, the Lord spoke to me and said, *You are healed!* I began rejoicing in my soul, continuously saying, "Thank You, Jesus! Thank You, Jesus!" I praised Him so much that I didn't even know when I finally fell asleep.

The next morning around 8:00 a.m., the doctor and his nurse arrived to check on me. Of course, they had no idea that their day would be anything but normal. Something unusual had happened during the night—it was a miracle!

The doctor approached my bed with his crisp white jacket, chart in hand, and a nurse by his side. He had a nice, gentle, compassionate smile that said to me, "I'm so sorry for your unfortunate accident."

"Eula, how are you doing?"

I responded, "I'm doing fine, doctor. How are you?"

He looked somewhat surprised, for how could I be so happy knowing that I would spend the rest of my life in a wheelchair? What he didn't know was that while he had been asleep or busy elsewhere, I had had a divine visitor.

The doctor had that look in his eyes, and before he could respond, I said to him, "Doctor, I'm healed." He looked at me with sadness, compassion, and pity, probably thinking I was in denial. He stated, "Eula, I'm sorry; I know you want to walk, but it's not possible because of that terrible accident!"

I looked at him and said, "Doctor, I can walk; the Lord has touched and healed me. And if you remove the IVs from my body, I will prove to you that God is a healer."

He stated, "I have surgery this morning, but as soon as I'm finished, I'll be back."

I replied, "I'll be waiting."

Around 10:00 a.m., the doctor and his nurse returned to my room—it was show time. He walked into the room as if to say, "Now let's finish where we left off earlier." I once again told him that if he removed the IVs, I would prove to him that God was a healer. At that, the nurse began removing the instruments and the IVs. When she was done, I stood in the center of the floor. God was gradually revealing His miraculous healing power because He said to me, *Put your left foot out.* Now, you must remember that because I was paralyzed, there was no feeling from waist down, so the best that I could do was *think* left. But as soon as I thought *left*, my left leg moved, God then said, *Now put your right foot out*, and I proceeded to move my right foot by faith, just as I had done with the left foot, and it moved. Again, God said, *Now put your left foot out again.* By this time, I began to feel like someone was sticking pins in my body from the waist down. It was life returning to my dead limbs; those legs that they said would never walk again! Again God said, *Now put your left foot out*, and when I did that, God said, *Walk!* I began walking as if nothing had ever happened to me.

The doctor was spellbound; he could not believe what had just happened. He showed me the X-ray and said, "See right here? You can't walk, you are paralyzed." I looked at him and said, "Doctor, I told you earlier that I was healed." He responded, "This truly is a miracle." I asked him to do one last thing for me, which was to put a postscript at the end of my chart that said "Eula says 'God is a healer.'"

I was determined that I was not going to live the rest of my days in a wheelchair; I was too young, and I had too many places to go and too many people to see. Negative thoughts bring about negative results; positive thoughts bring positive results. I wonder what you would accomplish if you just took control of your thoughts and decided *I can do this*! The mind is a powerful tool. Life and death is in the power of the tongue; you must speak it—go ahead, *speak it*. Tell yourself "I'm coming out this," "I'm not going out like this." Go ahead, talk to yourself; program your words to be positive. You can do it! You may say, "What if nothing happens?" Try it again. Jesus prayed three times; if the Savior prayed three times, what about us? Come on; speak it out loud so you can hear yourself! Now, let's take a look at the power of thoughts.

Chapter 3
The Power of Thought

For as he thinketh in his heart, so is he.

(Proverbs 23:7)

All that a man achieves and all that he fails to achieve
is the direct result of his own thoughts.

—James Allen

How and from where does thought power emerge? It is hidden in the subliminal cores of our minds. The human mind is indeed a majestic bequest of the Supreme Creator. However advanced it may be, no supercomputer of the world could ever equal nature's masterpiece—the human brain.

Have you ever given much thought with regard to what your thoughts are, where they come from, or the power they have in molding and shaping your life? Have you ever considered the fact that your thoughts are derived from and triggered as the result of pure consciousness? If you're like the vast majority, the answer is no. That's what we'll be looking at here—the power of thoughts, or more specifically, the power of your individual thoughts and the crucial role they play in determining how *every* event, condition, and circumstance in your life unfolds as a result of their creative power. Although it isn't the power of your thoughts alone that determines how things unfold, your chosen thoughts combined with the power of emotions that these chosen thoughts ignite, most certainly do.

You can really begin to appreciate the role that the power of your thoughts plays, which at the same time, when you learn to consciously direct the emotions that your thoughts ignite, you will begin to understand and see in a real and tangible way what a profound and transformational difference your individual mind power plays in the process.

Developing a crystal clear understanding as to how the power of thoughts affect every area of your life will serve to provide not only the desired outcomes experienced in your physical world, but it will give you unfailing and timeless wisdom that will provide *immense* benefit toward enhancing your mental, emotional, and spiritual growth and understanding, and provide a sense of peace, well-being, and overall fulfillment in every aspect of life as well. As you'll soon discover, *anything* and *everything* in the world begins and happens as a result of the power of thoughts. The predominant thoughts that you choose to think combined with the emotions that these chosen thoughts create will, with unwavering certainty, mold and shape your life physically, financially, relationally, emotionally, and spiritually.

Thought is quite literally the often overlooked seed that shapes your external world. Think deeply about this for a minute. Had Alexander Graham Bell not *thought* that he could invent a device that would allow you to pick up a device with numerous holes in each end, one that you could hear from and talk into, as well as transmit your voice thousands of miles in lightning-fast time, you wouldn't have the convenience of, or ability to, pick up the telephone and talk to someone on the other side of the world. If the Wright Brothers hadn't first conceived the *thought* that they could create a machine that would allow people to seemingly defy the law of gravity, we wouldn't know what it was like, or be able to board an airplane with the ability to travel from one side of the country to the other in a matter of a few hours.

Now, obviously the above examples were not just thought into existence. They are mentioned to express the importance of the power of thoughts, or more specifically, the conceptualization of a particular thought that serves as the seed that initiated the process for these things to be made real. But, had the seed never been planted, the harvest would not and could not exist. Once the seed is planted, it does have to be nurtured in order to reach full maturity.

But the whole process begins at the level of consciousness. It's consciousness that enables a thought to be thought initially.

Consciousness is the spiritual (or if you prefer, the unseen) realm, and thought is the first step in the process that makes all this "spiritual stuff" real and tangible. Without the power of thought, you have no power.

Also we must watch that group we hang out with. The older people used to say, "Birds of a feather flock together." Paul puts it this way: "Be not deceived: evil communications corrupt good manners" (1 Corinthians 15:33). Stop and think for a moment about the different people in your life. Your family, friends, colleagues, people you work with, etc. By listening to what they say, you can come pretty close to determining what their predominant thought patterns are and begin to develop a deeper understanding of how the power of thoughts fits into each individual circumstance.

Do you know of anyone who continually talks negatively about a specific relationship that they are in? Again, I can assure you that the relationship that they continually express dissatisfaction with is lacking in some way. That too is the power of thoughts in action. Now think about someone who constantly talks or worries about being ill. You can bet they are ill a great deal of the time. They get the flu every time the flu comes around. They get a cold every time they're exposed to the virus, etc.

Now let's shift gears a bit. How about someone that you know who is positive and upbeat all the time? In the same respect, their results in life will show it. Their external outcomes (events, conditions, and circumstances in life) are a direct reflection of their internal thought processes. All of these outcomes are excellent examples of the power of thoughts in action. Until the consistent, self-limiting thought process is changed that created the situation initially, the exact same results will continue. This pattern will continue to repeat itself over and over and over again until the thought process is changed and a different belief is established which will automatically attract the resources or conditions required for a different outcome!

How Does the Power of Thoughts Attract the Events, Conditions, and Circumstances That You Experience in Your Life?

Understanding and consciously directing the power of thoughts is what will shape *your* world in a way that you desire. Here's what gives the power of thoughts their "power."

Thoughts are a living, vibrating mass of energy packets (photons) that are every bit as real and alive as you and I. They cannot be sensed or experienced with the five basic human senses of hearing, sight, smell, touch, or taste. But they are certainly real, and will ultimately determine your success (or the lack of) in life.

Your whole existence and everything that you experience in your day-to-day life is brought about solely on what has recently been labeled the law of attraction. It is also known by other names such as *sowing and reaping* (in the Christian community), *Karma* (Buddhist), or as science refers to it, cause and effect. What you choose to call it is immaterial. All are one and the same and act in exact accordance with how the universe was created to operate.

There are a number of people in the world today who would nitpick and argue about which of these labels is correct. What they would find if they chose to delve deeper, keep an open mind, eliminate judgmental thinking, and investigate the reasoning and deeper meaning behind each, is that *they are all one and the same*, and *each of them is absolutely correct*!

Our current and ancestral spiritual teachers as well as the many great spiritual writings available to us clearly tell us that whatever it is we sow (or do), we will reap (receive) accordingly. What does that have to do with the power of thoughts? The thought is literally the "seed" that you are sowing, and emotion is the "fertilizer" that feeds and nourishes the originally conceived thought seed.

In Buddhist teachings, the law of Karma says this: For every event that occurs (initial act), there will follow another event whose existence was caused by the first, and this second event (the outcome) will be pleasant or unpleasant based on the skillfulness or the unskillfulness of the act which caused it.

What does this have to do with the power of thoughts? The thought acts as the cause of the event. Nothing can happen unless a thought is first conceived. Science states that for every cause (action), there must be an equal effect (outcome). Again, the thought acts as the cause.

The only difference in these three concepts is in the presentation or delivery, and the perception of the hearer. While many have heard these various truths, the majority only relate them to visible physical activity and fail to look deeply enough to develop the understanding that in order for a physical activity to happen, it must first begin as a thought or consciousness (the cause). When you begin to truly grasp this, you begin to clearly see and understand the creative power of thought and how it can and does impact every aspect of your life.

As mentioned earlier, anything and everything that has been created, is being created, or ever will be created is the result of consciousness, a process that begins as an unseen metaphysical or spiritual event which is stirred, and the process of creation is initiated by the power of thoughts. The bottom line is, *your* thoughts are the initial unseen seeds that determine the outcomes that you will experience in the physical world. Just as you plant a seed in the soil, it must surely produce a plant of similarity to the seed that was planted. If you were to plant crabgrass seeds, you certainly couldn't expect them to produce a big, beautiful oak tree. If you plant crabgrass seeds, you get crabgrass. If you plant an apple seed, you grow an apple tree. This simple universal principle is known to all. Even a young child understands it. With that being true, why would it be any different with our thoughts? ... It isn't!

That is great news! Why? Because by developing an understanding of this simple principle, by becoming conscious of the consistent thoughts that we choose to think, we can then go to work on restructuring and implementing the power of thoughts—more specifically, *your thoughts*—to begin to create *your life* based on your newly found knowledge and begin producing desired results. Just as you would plant the apple seed and grow an apple tree, whatever thought seeds that you release into the universe must bring back to you in physical form *exactly* what you planted.

No more than you would expect a crabgrass seed to produce an oak tree, can anyone expect the seed thoughts which create doubt, fear, lack, and limitation to produce a harvest of abundance and happiness in your life. By the same token, if you choose to plant thought seeds which project and create love, joy, peace, fulfillment, contentment, prosperity, etc., you will experience (reap) the harvest of your seeds that harmonize with the original seeds planted.

As in the examples above, these same principles are what determine your health and wellness. If your thoughts are constantly focused on health and wellness in your body, you will reap a harvest of health and wellness. If you are constantly focused on sickness and disease or a fear of such, the universe will return to you exactly what it is you asked it for: a body full of sickness and disease ("dis-ease").

It doesn't matter what the situation or circumstance, whether it be health, finances, relationships, etc. The power of thoughts is every bit as creative in health situations as it is with money matters. The power of thoughts—more specifically the power of *your* thoughts—combined with the emotional response that you choose as a result of these thoughts are equally as creative and powerful in your personal relationships as they are in any other part of your life. Your control over the power of thoughts can only be determined by your willingness to accept the fact that it's true and become consciously aware of the thoughts you choose to think.

The following information will expand on what we have just covered:

Change your thoughts, and you will change your world!

Make a conscious and consistent effort, and you will develop the ability to focus the power of thoughts on creating a life far in excess of what you may have previously conceived or believed was possible for you. You'll personally see and experience the transformational power that the power of thoughts can, does, and will provide.

The average human thinks 60,000 thoughts per day.

Whether you are conscious of it or not, you think an average of 60,000 thoughts per day. Isn't that amazing? The human mind thinks an average of 42 thoughts per minute. I think you'll agree, that is *a lot* of thinking. This is why it is so important to become conscious of and clearly understand the power of thoughts and become consciously aware of what *your* thoughts are attracting into your world.

Just as the thought vibration (spiritual) began and created a physical reaction in your brain, so the resulting vibrations intensified by an emotion will seek out and attract like or harmonious vibrations which vibrate at the same frequency, resulting in creation or a physical reaction in your external world.

The sad thing is this. Most people go from day to day throughout their lives not only totally unaware of the power of thoughts in producing the lives they desire, but what is equally as sad, is the fact that they aren't consciously aware of exactly what it is they are thinking!

In fact, 95 percent of the average person's thoughts are being thought unconsciously. By being unaware of or unconscious about what it is they're thinking, they are leaving to chance what they are producing (harvest) through their thinking!

Understand the laws of thought

Every man should have a comprehensive understanding of the laws of thought and their operations. Then alone can one live in this world smoothly and happily. He can utilize the helping forces to serve his ends in the best possible manner. He can neutralize the hostile forces or antagonistic currents. Just as the fish swims against the current, so also he will be able to go against the hostile currents by adjusting himself properly and safeguarding through suitable precautionary methods. Otherwise he becomes a slave. He is tossed about hither and thither helplessly by various currents. He is adrift like a wooden plank in a river. He is very miserable and unhappy always, although he is wealthy and possesses everything.

The captain of a steamer who has mariner's compass, who has knowledge of the sea, the routes, and the oceanic currents can sail smoothly. Otherwise his steamer will be drifted here and there helplessly and wrecked by dashing against some icebergs or rocks. Likewise, a wise sailor in the ocean of this life who has a detailed knowledge of the laws of thought and nature can sail smoothly and reach the goal of his life positively.

Understanding the laws of thought, you can mould or shape your character in any way you like. The common saying, "As a man thinketh so he becometh," is one of the great laws of thought. Think you are pure, pure you will become. Think you are noble, noble you will become.

Thought excels light in speed

While light travels at the rate of 186,000 miles per second, thoughts virtually travel in no time. Thought is finer than ether, the medium of electricity. In broadcasting, a singer sings beautiful songs in Calcutta. You can hear them nicely through the radio set in your own house at Delhi. All messages are received through the wireless.

Even so, your mind is like a wireless machine. A saint with peace, poise, harmony, and spiritual waves sends out into the world thoughts of harmony and peace. They travel with lightning speed in all directions and enter the minds of persons and produce in them also similar thoughts of harmony and peace. Whereas a worldly man whose mind is full of jealousy, revenge, and hatred sends out discordant thoughts which enter the minds of thousands and stir in them similar thoughts of hatred and discord.

The medium through which thoughts travel

If we throw a piece of stone in a tank or a pool of water, it will produce a succession of concentric waves traveling all around from the affected place. The light of a candle will similarly give rise to waves of ethereal vibrations traveling in all directions from the candle. In the same manner, when a thought, whether good or evil, crosses the mind of a person, it gives rise to vibrations in the Manas or mental atmosphere, which travel far and wide in all directions. What is the possible medium through which thoughts can travel from one mind to another? The best possible explanation is that Manas, or mind-substance, fills all space like ether and it serves as the vehicle for thoughts, as Prana is the vehicle for feeling, as ether is the vehicle for heat, light, and electricity, and as air is the vehicle for sound.

Thoughts are living things

Thoughts are living things. A thought is as much solid as a piece of stone. We may cease to be, but our thoughts can never die. Every change in thought is accompanied by vibration of its matter (mental). Thought as force needs a special kind of subtle matter in its working. The stronger the thoughts, the earlier the fructification. Thought is focused and given a particular direction and, in the degree that thought is thus focused and given direction, it is effective in the work it is sent out to accomplish.

Thoughts as wireless messages

Those who harbour thoughts of hatred, jealousy, revenge, and malice are very dangerous persons. They cause unrest and ill will amongst men. Their thoughts and feelings are like wireless messages broadcast in ether, and are received by those whose minds respond to such vibrations.

Thought moves with tremendous velocity. Those who entertain sublime and pious thoughts help others who are in their vicinity and at a distance also.

Thoughts are tremendous powers

Thought has got tremendous power. Thought can heal diseases. Thoughts can transform the mentality of persons. Thought can do anything. It can work wonders. The velocity of thought is unimaginable. Thought is a dynamic force. It is caused by the vibrations of psychic Prana or Sukshma Prana on the mental substance. It is a force like gravitation, cohesion, or repulsion. Thought travels or moves.

Thought—its power, workings, and uses

Thought is a vital, living dynamic power—the most vital, subtle, and irresistible force existing in the universe. Through the instrumentality of thought, you acquire creative power. Thought passes from one man to another. It influences people; a man of powerful thought can influence readily people of weak thoughts.

There are nowadays numerous books on thought-culture, thought power, thought-dynamics. A study of them will give you a comprehensive understanding of thought, its power, its workings, and usefulness.

We live in a boundless world of thoughts

Thought alone is the whole world, the great pains, the old age, death and the great sin, earth, water, fire, air, ether. Thought binds a man. He who has controlled his thoughts is a veritable God on this earth.

You live in a world of thoughts. First is thought. Then there is the expression of that thought through the organ of speech. Thought and language are intimately connected. Thoughts of anger, bitterness, and malice injure others. If the mind, which is the cause of all thoughts vanishes, the external objects will disappear.

Thoughts are things. Sound, touch, form, taste, and odour, the five sheaths, the waking, the dreaming, and deep sleep states—all these are the products of mind. Sankalpa, passion, anger, bondage, time—know them to be the result of mind. Mind is the king of the Indriyas or senses. Thought is the root of all mental process.

The thoughts that we perceive all round us are only the mind in form or substance. Thought creates, thought destroys. Bitterness and sweetness do not lie in the objects, but they are in the mind, in the subject, in thinking. They are created by thought.

Through the play of the mind or thought upon objects, proximity appears to be a great distance and vice versa. All objects in this world are unconnected; they are connected and associated together only by thought, by the imagination of your mind. It is the mind that gives colour, shape, and qualities to the objects. Mind assumes the shape of any object it intensely thinks upon.

Friend and enemy, virtue and vice are in the mind only. Every man creates a world of good and evil, pleasure and pain, out of his own imagination only. Good and evil, pleasure and pain do not proceed from objects. These belong to the attitude of your mind. There is nothing good nor pleasant in this world. Your imagination makes it so.

Your eyes betray your thoughts

The eyes which represent the windows of the soul bespeak of the condition and state of the mind. There is a telegraphic instrument in the eyes to transmit the messages or thoughts of treachery, depression, gloom, hatred, cheerfulness, peace, harmony, health, power, strength, and beauty.

If you have the faculty to read the eyes of others, you can read the mind at once. You can read the uppermost thought or dominant thought of a man if you are careful to mark the signs in his face, conversation, and behaviour. It needs a little pluck, acumen, training, intelligence, and experience.

Negative thoughts poison life

Thoughts of worry and thoughts of fear are fearful forces within us. They poison the very sources of life and destroy the harmony, the running efficiency, the vitality, and vigour. While the opposite thoughts of cheerfulness, joy and courage, heal, soothe, instead of irritating, and immensely augment efficiency and multiply the mental powers. Be always cheerful. Smile. Laugh.

Psycho-physical imbalances

Thought exerts its influence over the body. Grief in the mind weakens the body. Body influences the mind also in its turn. A healthy body makes the mind healthy. If the body is sick, the mind also becomes sick. If the body is strong and healthy, the mind also becomes healthy and strong.

Violent fits of hot-temper do serious damage to the brain cells, throw poisonous chemical products into the blood, produce general shock and depression and suppress the secretion of gastric juice, bile, and other digestive juices in the alimentary canal, drain away your energy, vitality, induce premature old age and shorten life.

When you are angry, the mind becomes disturbed. Similarly, when the mind is disturbed, the body also becomes disturbed. The whole nervous system is agitated. You become enervated. Control anger by love. Anger is a powerful energy that is uncontrollable by practical Vyavaharic Buddhi, but controllable by pure reason (Sattvic Buddhi) or Viveka-Vichara.

The creative powers of thought

Thought creates the world. Thought brings things into existence. Thoughts develop the desires and excite the passions. So, the contrary thoughts of killing the desires and passions will counteract the former idea of satisfying the desires. So when a person is impressed with this, a contrary thought will help him to destroy his desires and passions.

Think of a person as a good friend of yours and there the thing is created as a reality. Think of him as your foe, and then also the mind perfects the thought into an actuality. He who knows the workings of the mind and has controlled it by practice is really happy.

Similar thoughts attract each other

In the thought-world also, the great law "Like attracts like" operates. People of similar thoughts are attracted towards each other. That is the reason why the maxims run as follows: "Birds of the same feather flock together," "A man is known by the company he keeps."

A doctor is drawn towards a doctor. A poet has attraction for another poet. A songster loves another songster. A philosopher likes another philosopher. A vagabond likes a vagabond. The mind has got a "drawing power." You are continually attracting towards you, from both the seen and the unseen sides of life-forces, thoughts, influences, and conditions most akin to those of your own thoughts and lines.

In the realm of thought, people of similar thoughts are attracted to one another. This universal law is continually operating whether we are conscious of it or not. Carry any kind of thought you please about with you and so long as you retain it, no matter how you roam over the land or sea, you will unceasingly attract to yourself, knowingly or inadvertently, exactly and only what corresponds to your own dominant quality of thought. Thoughts are your private property and you can regulate them to suit your taste entirely by steadily recognizing your ability to do so.

You have entirely in your own hands to determine the order of thought you entertain and consequently the order of influence you attract and are not mere willowy creatures of circumstances, unless indeed you choose to be.

Spanish Flu and the contagion of thoughts

Mental actions are real actions. Thought is the real action; it is a dynamic force. It may be remembered, thought is very contagious; nay, more contagious than the Spanish Flu. A sympathetic thought in you raises a sympathetic thought in others with whom you come in contact. A thought of anger produces a similar vibration in those who surround an angry man. It leaves the brain of one man and enters the brains of others who live at a long distance and excites them.

A cheerful thought in you produces cheerful thoughts in others. You are filled with joy and intense delight when you see a batch of hilarious children playing mirthfully and dancing in joy. A thought of joy in us creates sympathetically a thought of joy in others. So do sublime elevating thoughts. Keep a good and honest man in the company of a thief. He will begin to steal. Keep a sober man in the company of a drunkard. He will begin to drink. Thought is very contagious.

The application of a psychological law

Keep the heart young. Do not think: "I have become old." To think "I have become old" is a bad habit. Do not entertain this thought.

At 60, think "I am 16." As you think, so you become. This is a great psychological law. "As a man thinketh so he becometh." This is a great truth or truism. Think, "I am strong," strong you become. Think, "I am weak," weak you become. Think, "I am a fool," fool you become. Think, "I am a sage or God," sage or God you become.

Thought alone shapes and moulds a man. Man lives always in a world of thoughts. Every man has his own thought-world. Imagination works wonders. Thought has tremendous force. Thought as already said, is a solid thing. Your present is the result of your past thoughts and your future will be according to your present thoughts. If you think rightly, you will speak rightly and act rightly. Speech and action simply follow the thoughts.

Thought–a boomerang

Be careful of your thoughts. Whatever you send out of your mind comes back to you. Every thought you think, is a boomerang. If you hate another, hate will come back to you. If you love others, love will come back to you.

An evil thought is thrice cursed. First, it harms the thinker by doing injury to his mental body. Secondly, it harms the person who is its object. Lastly, it harms all mankind by vitiating the whole mental atmosphere. Every evil thought is as a sword drawn on the person to whom it is directed. If you entertain thoughts of hatred, you are really a murderer of that man against whom you foster thoughts of hatred. You are your own suicide, because these thoughts rebound upon you only. A mind tenanted by evil thoughts acts as a magnet to attract like thoughts from others and thus intensifies the original evil. Evil thoughts thrown into the mental atmosphere poison receptive minds. To dwell on an evil thought gradually deprives it of its repulsiveness and impels the thinker to perform an action which embodies it.

> Do not under estimate the Power of Thoughts. Just as water has the power to shift and mold earth's landscape, your thoughts have the power to shift and mold the landscape of your life.
>
> —Chuck Danes

"Become consciously aware of what you're thinking about, and change the focus of those thoughts to what you desire to create for your life." Sounds simple doesn't it? Don't let the simplicity of this principle fool you. It is extremely powerful! The really good news is that you *do* have control over your thoughts. Your thoughts, once you learn to become consciously aware of them, do not have control over you. You are in *complete* control of them. Your thoughts do not think you; you think your thoughts.

Chapter 4
What to Do While I'm Waiting

Teach us, O Lord, the disciplines of patience, for to wait is often harder than to work.

—Peter Marshall

How do you handle yourself while waiting on God to bring something to pass? What do I do in the meanwhile? Getting involved and doing something while waiting on your deliverance will cause you to shift your thinking to something other than your situation. In the same way you occupy yourself while waiting in the doctor's office or your plane to board or standing in the grocery line, you find something or somebody that you can focus on. And the more you focus on others and less on yourself, the waiting period becomes smaller. It's your turn before you realize it. The same scenario holds true when waiting on your deliverance from God. As Peter Marshall states, "When we long for life without difficulties, remind us that oaks grow strong in contrary winds and diamonds are made under pressure." The enemy desires that you only think of your situation and not from the prospective that you are a diamond in the rough.

Learn how to occupy yourself while waiting for deliverance. Listed below are things you can do while you are waiting:

Praise the Lord

- Christians glorify God. We praise God because of *who* He is, and *what* He has done for us.

- We praise God because He is great and powerful. "For the Lord is great and greatly to be praised" (Psalm 96:4). "Be exalted, O LORD, in Your own strength! We will sing and praise Your power" (Psalm 21:13).

- We glorify God because He is righteous: "And my tongue shall speak of Your righteousness and of Your praise all the day long" (Psalm 35:28). "I will praise the LORD according to His righteousness, and will sing praise to the name of the LORD Most High" (Psalm 7:17).

- We glorify God because He is faithful and true: "O LORD, You are my God. I will exalt You, I will praise Your name, for You have done wonderful things; Your counsels of old are faithfulness and truth" (Isaiah 25:1).

- We praise God because of His mercy: "Praise the LORD, for His mercy endures forever" (2 Chronicles 20:21). "Praise the Lord! Oh, give thanks to the LORD, for He is good! For His mercy endures forever" (Psalm 106:1). "Oh, praise the LORD, all you Gentiles! Laud Him, all you peoples! For His merciful kindness is great toward us, and the truth of the LORD endures forever. Praise the Lord!" (Psalm 117:1–2).

- "Make a joyful shout to the LORD, all you lands! Serve the LORD with gladness; come before His presence with singing. Know that the LORD, He is God; it is He who has made us, and not we ourselves; we are His people and the sheep of His pasture. Enter into His gates with thanksgiving, and into His courts with praise. Be thankful to Him, and bless His name. For the LORD is good; His mercy is everlasting, and His truth endures to all generations" (Psalm 100:1–5).

- "You are my God, and I will praise You; You are my God, I will exalt You. Oh, give thanks to the LORD, for He is good! For His mercy endures forever" (Psalm 118:28–29).

- We praise God because He saves us. "The LORD is my strength and song, and He has become my salvation; He is my God, and

I will praise Him" (Exodus 15:2). "The Lord lives! Blessed be my Rock! Let God be exalted, the Rock of my salvation!" (2 Samuel 22:47). "Sing to the Lord, all the earth; proclaim the good news of His salvation from day to day. Declare His glory among the nations, His wonders among all peoples. For the Lord is great and greatly to be praised" (1 Chronicles 16:23–25). "The Lord lives! Blessed be my Rock! Let the God of my salvation be exalted" (Psalm 18:46). Amen.

Fast

Fasting is refraining from food for a spiritual purpose. It has always been a normal part of a relationship with God; it brings you into a deeper, more intimate and powerful relationship with the Lord. When you eliminate food from your diet for a number of days, your spirit becomes uncluttered by the things of this world and amazingly sensitive to the things of God. Whether you desire to be closer to God or are in need of great breakthroughs in your life, nothing shall be impossible to you. The Bible records many different circumstances, types, and lengths of fasts. Joshua fasted forty days, Daniel fasted twenty-one days, and apostle Paul was on at least two fasts: one for three days and one for fourteen days. Peter fasted three days, and of course Jesus fasted forty days in the wilderness.

There are three types of fasts found in the Bible: absolute fast, the normal fast, and the partial fast.

> **Absolute fast**—is extreme and should be done only for very short periods of time. On an absolute fast, you take in nothing—no food nor water. Depending on your health, this fast should be attempted only with medical consultation and supervision.

> **Normal fast**—you typically go without food of any kind for a certain number of days. You do drink water, and plenty of it! Depending on the length of the normal fast, you may choose to take clear broth and juices in order to maintain your strength.

> **Partial fast**—can be interpreted many ways. The way

it cannot be interpreted is to include that time between 11:00 p.m. and 6:00 a.m. when you're sleeping! A partial fast usually involves giving up particular foods and drink for an extended period of time. The *Daniel fast*—eliminating meat, bread, and sweets for twenty-one days. I think this one just about anyone can handle. Some think eliminating only those three foods from your diet for three weeks is no big deal. But if it means something to you, it will mean something to God. After all, when was the last time angels were released to speak mysteries to you like the archangel Michael spoke to Daniel?

Since the Daniel fast has become somewhat popular over the last few years among believers, let's take a brief look at it. This example is only to give you a general idea of the procedure.

Purpose

God is calling for us to turn from our wicked ways and return unto Him. Throughout the Bible, whenever God's people came before Him with fasting and prayer, *something miraculous happened to and for them.* All believers should fast but no regulations or set rules are given as to how long or how often one should fast. That is determined by one's desire and need (Matthew 9:14–15; 1 Corinthians 7:5; Acts 13:1–5).

Read the stories where God was sought through fasting in these Scriptures.

1. **Deliverance:** Esther 4:16. Esther and the Jews fasting and praying for God's help on her dangerous mission, going in to see the king on behalf of her people.
2. **Guidance and protection:** Ezra 8:21–23. Ezra and the children of Israel fasted and prayed asking God to show them the right way and for protection as they traveled through dangerous and difficult territory.
3. **Directions:** Nehemiah 1:4–11. Upon hearing the tragic news about Jerusalem, Nehemiah fasted and prayed to God for the people of Israel. God gave him ways to move beyond his grief to specific actions to help his people.

4. **Under chastening:** 2 Samuel 12:16–23. When David's sin (taking Uriah's wife, Bathsheba; and having Uriah killed) was exposed. David repented, God forgave him but he was chastised (the Lord struck the child Bathsheba bore with sickness). Before the child died David besought God through fasting. After the death of the child, David was able to get up, wash and anoint himself, change his clothes, go to the house of the Lord and worship him, go back home, eat, talk to his friends, and comfort his wife.

5. **Under judgment:** 1 Kings 21:29. Jezebel plotted to get Naboth's vineyard for Ahab. Under wicked instructions the elders of the city proclaimed a fast and followed Jezebel's instructions to have Naboth killed so Ahab could get his vineyard. The prophet Elijah announced doom on Ahab and Jezebel. However, when judgment came Ahab humbled himself and fasted. Because Ahab humbled himself God did not bring evil in his days; but on his son's days.

6. **When worried:** Daniel 6:18. Darius the king wanted so much to deliver Daniel but his efforts were in vain. The king went through the night fasting. He rose early in the morning and went in haste to the den of lions to check on Daniel.

7. **In trouble:** Acts 27:9. Paul was sent to Rome and confronted contrary winds at sea.

8. **In spiritual conflict:** Matthew 4:1–11. Jesus fasted 40 days and 40 nights and was afterward tempted by the devil.

9. **Desperate in prayer:** Acts 9. Saul/Damascus didn't eat or drink. The Lord spoke to Ananias in a vision and sent him to Saul.

Fasting has both spiritual and physical benefits.

Spiritual benefits: Increased faith, salvation, deliverance, righteous in lifestyle, humbling, strengthen the inner (spiritual) man, closer walk with the Lord, holy living, peace, contentment and a satisfied soul, guidance, and prosperity.

Physical benefits: Healing and strength in the body; fasting helps cleanse your body of toxic wastes which accumulate in your spiritual and physical body. You may become irritable or short-tempered.

Instructions

1. If you are on medication or have health problems, check with your physician for advice and consult with the Great Physician before attempting this fast.
2. Read the Scriptures daily, pray and mediate on them.
3. Repent to God for known and unknown sins. Ask God to renew a right spirit within you.
4. Be a blessing to others, help those in need. Pray for others. Be faithful to church.
5. Abstain from soft drinks, coffee, tea, desserts, sweets, candy, breads, meats, milk, Gatorade, snack foods, TV, idle talk, bad company, non-Christian music and programs, computer games, Play Stations, etc.
6. Keep praise in your heart throughout the day and night. Avoid unhealthy conversation. You are on a Holy Fast unto the Lord.
7. Why are you fasting? *Be specific about what you want God to do or what you want to do for God.* Believe God. Your fast is a statement of faith in God. Faith is foundational to fasting.
8. *Pray, pray, pray.* Constant prayer reflects your level of *spiritual commitment* during the fast. Pray without ceasing. Set aside a prayer time during the day or the night.
9. This is a 24-hour 7-day-a-week fast for 21 days.
10. Hold to whatever *time commitment* you make to God in regard to this fast. If you set your heart to fast 21 days, don't stop on the 15th day.
11. *Consult with the pastor* for prayer and make sure you consult with your physician before starting this fast.
12. Exercise, walk the length of your home (inside), seven times each morning and night swinging your arms and praising God for answering your prayers (Isaiah 65:21–24).
13. *Testimony commitment.* Leave the results of your fasting and praying up to God. Watch God move on your behalf, in your situations, or concerning the specific needs you've given to him. Be ready to share your testimony with others.

Menu—Consume these nutrients as often as you like.

Week 1: water, fruit juices, broth, fruits, soups, nuts, salads, chowder, crackers, Jell-O, vegetables

Week 2: water, fruit juices, soups, fruits, nuts, salads, beans, vegetables, crackers, Jell-O

Week 3: water, fruit juices, soups, fruits, beans, nuts, salads, vegetables, nonfried foods

Description	Week	Date	Scripture(s)
Sincerity	1	1	Isaiah 1:16–18
Obedience		2	Isaiah 1:19–20
		3	Isaiah 59:1–2
			Romans 3:23; 6:23
Confession		4	Revelation 3:15–19
			Psalm 51:13
			Luke 18:9–14
Repent		5	Revelation 3:2–3
			Acts 2:37–38
			Hebrews 12:5–17
Covenant		6	2 Chronicles 15:12–15
Commitment		7	2 Chronicles 15:2; 7:14
Justified	2	8	Romans 3:24; 5:1–2, 9
Hold Fast		9	Revelations 3:10–11
Saved		10	Romans 3:34; 10:9–10
Spiritual Life		11	Romans 8:5–15
			Acts 1:8
Abide		12	John 15:1–7
Work		13	Ecclesiastes 9:10
			Matthew 20:1–16
			2 Thessalonians 3:10
			Proverbs 19:15
Stewardship		14	Matthew 25:14–30
Holiness	3	15	1 Peter 1:13–21
			Hebrews 12:14; Psalm 15
Integrity		16	Proverbs 20:7; 19:1

Description	Week	Date	Scripture(s)
Study		17	2 Timothy 2:15
			1 Timothy 4:15–16
Forgiveness		18	Genesis 27:30–41
			Genesis 32:6–11; 32:1–4
Thankful		19	Luke 17:11–19
			Revelation 4:11
			Isaiah 51:11
Reward		20	2 Chronicles 15:7
			3 John 2
Desire		21	Psalm 19:7–14

- **Get involved with church/community activities.** Volunteer at one of local charitable organization: The Red Cross, Salvation Army, or even a church.

- **Exercise in a way that brings you joy.** In the long run, taking regular walks, hiking, playing with your kids, and tending to your home and garden will do more for your body and soul than a four-thousand-dollar weight machine you'd rather die than use.

- **Take a trip to a place you've always wanted to see.** If doing so means taking a little money out of your savings account, so be it. A few hundred bucks extra in the bank don't compare to the feeling of following a dream. Remember, the only things we take with us when we die are our lessons and memories. Make sure they're good ones!

- **Practice mindfulness.** In simplest terms, this means *being* in the moment, no matter what you're doing. The past is gone and the future is undefined, so don't let your mind dwell on things you do not have control of.

- **Play in a pile of leaves or sand.** Allowing your inner child to run wild now and then is not just fun, but also fulfills one of your soul's most basic needs—freedom. If the thought of tearing through your yard throwing leaves into the air seems a bit embarrassing to you, remember that your *soul* doesn't give a darn what the neighbors think, and neither should you!

- **Try free-writing.** You can do this either on your computer or the old-fashioned way, with pen and paper. Write without conscious thought and don't edit yourself. Just jot down anything that comes to mind, exactly as it comes to mind. At first, the resulting pages will sound like gibberish to you, but if you look a little closer, you'll find a certain grace to your words. The greater benefit of free-writing, of course, is that it may reveal some deep-seated emotions, beliefs, or fears you weren't even aware of and can then begin to work through. **Keep a dream journal.** Write down your dreams as soon as you wake up, in as much detail as possible. In time, you will notice distinct themes. These themes, along with their unique symbolisms and attached emotions, will soon enable you to better understand who you are as a person and as a soul.

- **Slow down your pace.** The best way to explain what I mean by this is to use the words of a spirit guide: Life should be a slow dance, not a seizure.

- **Don't be afraid of aging.** Wrinkles and gray hair are nothing to be ashamed of. Sure, you can use your various lotions and hair dyes, but don't panic every time you realize you're not twenty anymore, and don't abuse your body with poisons, pills, and endless surgeries in order to shave a few years off your appearance. To live in violent denial of your physical age is not healthy for your body, mind, *or* spirit.

- **Take an afternoon nap.** For some reason, dreams seem to be more vivid during naps than during regular sleep time. Take advantage of this phenomenon whenever possible—just don't do it at work or while piloting aircraft.

- **Explore another culture.** Whether it be through cuisine, dance, clothing, or traditions, open your mind and heart to the way of life of a totally foreign people. This promotes a sense of global unity and teaches us to be more tolerant.

- **Embrace change.** Life is not meant to be static. As we change, so does our reality. It is a normal process and should be celebrated, not feared.

- **Don't sweat the small stuff.** You've lived many lives; you've been both rich and poor, strong and weak, noble and petty, giving and greedy. You've seen wars, faced great violence, survived major disasters, and you've overcome obstacles you cannot begin to imagine. So when the baker gets the icing of your birthday cake wrong or you find a minor scratch on your car, don't blow a fuse. Take a deep breath, smile, and move on.

- **Let go of envy.** If others have more than you, remember that material possessions mean nothing in the grand scheme of things. Enjoy what you have and you'll be a much, much happier person.

- **Stop believing that the universe is picking on you.** I know sometimes it feels as though everyone is getting ahead except for you and that God plays favorites, but that simply isn't true. You are exactly where you need to be to learn the lessons you need to learn, and what you consider bad luck now may well turn out to be a blessing down the road. Do your best, and let the rest take care of itself.

- **Laugh more.** Laughter is immensely important for your overall well-being, so don't be afraid to be goofy or crack your own particular brand of jokes. Humor is a major aspect of self-expression; your level of self-expression tells much about your self-acceptance. Your level of self-acceptance, in turn, speaks volumes about your spiritual advancement.

- **Don't hold back your tears.** One of my spirit guides once asked me why humans try so hard not to cry. To be honest, I was stumped. Why *do* we do that? Why would we rather turn bright red, choke, sputter, and run away to hide in a dark corner than be seen with tears in our eyes? In the end, I think maybe it's foolish pride. We don't want to be viewed as weak or overly sentimental, so we go against our nature. Obviously, this isn't a good practice. Cry if you need to. There's no shame in tears.

- **Get to know God.** Even the best spouses fail; God never will. Take time to talk—and listen—to Him concerning your future. Meditate on verses about His faithfulness. Discover that human standards of "worthiness" mean nothing to Him; His affection is unconditional. When we make this pivotal truth our own, we can develop a *heavenly* confidence that permeates all we do.

- **Build a community.** Life is infinitely richer when we generate and nurture friendships. It's easy to develop tunnel vision and surround ourselves only with those who are "relationship material." Resist the urge. Dates come and go, but friends are God's arms, holding us up when romantic ventures let us down.

- **Do what you love.** Have you always been an artist at heart? When you run, do you "feel His pleasure"? The more we develop our talents—particularly if we use our skills to bring glory to God—the more we experience enthusiasm and joy, whatever our circumstances. (There's also something extremely attractive about a person with a passion for life!)

- **Discover something new.** Is there an instrument or language you want to learn? Have you dreamed of backpacking around Europe? This is your moment. When spouses and kids enter the picture, money will be allocated differently—so if you can afford to follow a dream, make it a priority. If money is tight, opportunities still abound. Increase your knowledge by researching online or at the library, or raise support to take a mission trip.

- **Help others.** A poet once wrote, "I sought my soul, but my soul I could not see. I sought my God, but my God eluded me. I sought my brother, and I found all three." Volunteer at a nursing home or soup kitchen. Be a mentor. Rake someone's leaves. When we're feeling empty, we benefit immeasurably by serving folks in need. As their strength is renewed, *our* cups overflow.

- **But don't compromise.** Funny what loneliness can do. People with whom we have nothing in common—and sometimes hardly *like*—are suddenly attractive. We can even convince ourselves it's unreasonable for God to make us wait for physical pleasure. But anytime we push ahead of Him, either by trying to force a dubious relationship or misplacing our moral compass, we're like the Prodigal Son, sifting through slop when we could revel in riches down the road.

God really desires to occupy your mind, and in essence when we come into the knowledge of ...

Waiting for God—He strengthens us

As you are waiting for God, He strengthens you. "But those who wait on the Lord will find new strength. They will fly high on wings as eagles. They will run and not grow weary. They will walk and not faint" (Isaiah 40:31).

God strengthens us during our trials. Did you know that an eagle knows when a storm is approaching long before it breaks? The eagle will fly to a high spot and wait for the winds to come. When the storm hits, it sets its wings so that the wind will pick it up and lift it above the storm. While the storm rages below, the eagle is soaring above it. The eagle does not escape the storm; it simply uses the storm to lift it higher. It rises on the winds that bring the storm. When the storms of life come upon us, we can rise above them by setting our minds and our belief toward God. The storms do not have to overcome us; we can allow God's power to lift us above them. God enables us to ride the winds of the storm that bring sickness, tragedy, failure, and disappointment into our lives. We can soar above the storm. It is my perception that it is not the burdens of life that weigh us down, it is how we handle them.

Waiting for God—He blesses us

When waiting for God, He blesses you. "Yet the LORD longs to be gracious to you; he rises to show you compassion. For the LORD is a God of justice. Blessed are all who wait for him" (Isaiah 30:18).

What does it mean to be blessed by God while we wait on Him? As we wait on God and His timing, He can accomplish so much in our hearts. Often we find new purpose in life, receive answers to prayer, see God work, increase our faith, and most often we see God's perfect plan fulfilled in our situation. Remember, waiting is not wasted time!

> Faith is an oasis in the heart which can never be reached
> by the caravan of thinking.
> —Kahlil Gibran

Chapter 5
Faith in Action

Faith is taking the first step even when you don't see the whole staircase.

—Martin Luther King Jr.

The adversary has launched his attack at the patience of the people of God, but "faith" is the bondage breaker! Faith is a powerful force which is proven by the Lord's declaration that it's able to move mountains. Faith is a complete trust, confidence, and reliance in God. It is a firm belief without proof, a yearning from the bottom of one's heart for God's Kingdom to come. It means absolute allegiance, loyalty, and fidelity to God no matter under what circumstances. Faith laughs and triumphs over impossibilities. For the writer of Hebrews lets us know, by faith, the warriors of the early church subdued kingdoms.

> "By faith passed through the Red sea as by dry land: which the Egyptians assaying to do were drowned. By Faith the walls of Jericho fell down, after they were compassed about seven days. Who through faith subdued kingdoms, wrought righteousness, obtained promises, stopped the mouths of lions"
> (Hebrews 11:29, 30, 33).

The apostle John also encourages us to believe that faith can overcome the world: "For whatsoever is born of God overcometh the world: and this is the victory that overcometh the world, even our faith" (1 John 5:4).

It is fitting to consider faith after repentance, seeing that true repentance merges into faith as the blossom ripens into fruit. Tears of sincere grief over sin lead to a saving trust in God. Without faith, repentance recedes into indifference or moves into hopeless remorse. Faith is vital in that it leads the repentant soul to God, first to receive His forgiveness and then to appropriate His resources for daily victory, holiness, and inspiration for effective service.

The importance of faith is indicated by the act that all men are dependent upon it as the avenue of access to God. Sinners, convicted of their need, must exercise faith in God as one ready to pardon them, if they are to be saved. Saints, saved by grace through faith in Christ, must continue to believe. For the Scripture states, "As you have therefore received Christ Jesus the Lord, so walk ye in him" (Colossians 2:6). Hopefully, your faith will be enhanced by the testimonies of the various individuals and with the information of this document.

Since the days of becoming a Christian, many things have changed. A few examples are: the music, dress, decor, activities that we can participate in, leadership, and others. When you see the drastic change, it causes one to question, "How long, oh Lord?" But the age-old reply returns, "He that will come, shall come and will not tarry." Preparation is not an option, but it's *essential*! For the Lord stated to His disciples, "Hardly will he find faith when he returns." The love of many has waxed cold, therefore leaving the people of God callous, aloof, and indifferent. Faith has always been the main ingredient for pleasing God and for developing a people for his namesake. Faith is one of the greatest qualities of a Christian's life. It is the foundation of the inner man that enables the building of hope, love, peace, and all other attributes of a life that is ordered by the will of God. Faith gives hope, meaning, and purpose to all knowledge. It is fundamental to our relationship with God. The only spiritual ingredient that supersedes faith is charity (1 Corinthians 13:13).

I trust that you will profit from this book. Its goal is to strengthen, inspire, and exhilarate. The enemy has devised a plan to attack the faith of Christians, but you must always keep in mind that "No weapon that is formed against you shall prosper." For our faith will carry us through!

Two words describe our faith: *confidence* and *certainty*. These two qualities need a secure beginning and ending point. The beginning point of faith is believing in God's character: He is who He says. The end point is believing in God's promises: He will do what He says. We believe that God will fulfill His promises even though we don't see those promises materializing now, for this is true faith. John 20:24–31 states:

> But Thomas, one of the twelve, called Didymus, was not with them when Jesus came. The other disciples therefore said unto him, We have seen the Lord. But he said unto them, Except I shall see in his hands the print of the nails, and put my finger into the print of the nails, and thrust my hand into his side, I will not believe. And after eight days, again his disciples were within, and Thomas with them: then came Jesus, the doors being shut, and stood in the midst, and said Peace be unto you. Then saith he to Thomas, *Reach hither thy finger, and behold my hands, and reach hither thy hand, and thrust it into my side; and be not faithless, but believing.* And Thomas answered and said unto him, My Lord and my God. Jesus said unto him, *Thomas because thou hast seen me, thou hast believed: blessed are they that have not seen, and yet have believed.* These are written, that ye might believe that Jesus is the Christ, the Son of God; and that believing ye might have life through his name. (emphasis added)

While Bible scholars have given us many descriptions of the nature of faith, the Bible itself has one definition only, if you can call it a definition. Often attempts to define faith only tend to make it more obscure. The writer of Hebrews (11:1) states that "faith is the substance of things hoped for: the evidence of things not seen." Arthur Way's translation is expressive: "Faith which issues in the winning of life. It is that attitude of mind which is the foundation-rock on which hope stands, that which satisfies us of the reality of things as yet beyond our ken." Noyes gives us this rendering: "Faith is the assurance of things hoped for, and conviction of things not seen." Dean Alford has it, "Faith is the confidence of things hoped for, the evidence of things not seen."

God's Spirit makes known in His Word certain things not seen and produces within the believer the conviction that these actually exist. Thus He endures as seeing things invisible. The substance of this Bible definition of faith is that of believing one is able to penetrate beyond the veil that marks the limit of sense and enters into the region of unseen things, making them tangible and real. Such faith is not mere human wisdom or sagacity but has its foundation in a spiritual understanding. It is the receiving of the testimony that it is true.

> Now faith is the substance of things hoped for, the evidence of things not seen.
>
> (Hebrews 11:1)

> God is not a man, that he should lie: neither the son of man, that he should repent: hath he said, and shall he not do it?
>
> (Numbers 23:19)

By faith Isaac blessed Jacob and Esau concerning things to come (Hebrews 11:20). It was this faith that stretched out its hands into the dim future and came back filled with a blessing that was in Moses's estimation of greater value than his flocks and herds. This is a faith that can lay hold of things in the unseen world now (Hebrews 11:26–27). To Moses, the unseen treasures made real to his faith, outweighed the crown, throne, and glory of Egypt.

In Dr. R. A. Torrey's monumental work *What the Bible Teaches*, he gives us this definition of faith:

> To believe God is to rely upon or have unhesitating assurance of the truth of God's testimony, even though it is unsupported by any other evidence, and to rely upon and have unfaltering assurance of the fulfillment of His promises, even though everything seems against fulfillment.

After purchasing the first twenty-five acres of land to build our church, we realized that we needed to purchase the land beside it to keep out unwanted purchasers whose goals or aims were not Christian oriented. Knowing we did not have the funds for the purchase, we needed to start negotiation for that piece of property. How in the name of the Lord, was I supposed to purchase this land with no funds? But as Kahlil Gibran said, "Faith is an oasis in the heart which can never be reached by the caravan of thinking."

Deciding to handle this, I called a friend who was in real estate and asked his advice. He informed me how to approach the situation, even down to my apparel. He told me the words to use as I talked with the owners, which briefcase to carry—the whole nine yards. I called the prayer warriors and told them the situation. They informed me "we are on it." I took two of my sisters with me and informed them to stay in the car and not stop praying until I returned. I walked into the office and announced myself and asked to speak with the president. I was asked by an associate if one of them could help me. I informed them they could not; I needed to speak to the person who owned the land, not a representative. I realized the representative could not give me what did not belong to them.

With that, the associate asked me to have a seat and disappeared, returning a few minutes later with a gentleman. He informed me he was the president of the company and invited me to his office. Arriving at his office; he asked what he could do for me. (He was about to find out.)

I informed him that we had purchased twenty-five acres of land from him, and I was there to ask him to give us the fifteen acres adjunct to the land we had previously purchased. For a moment he was totally spellbound. He finally came out of shock as he stood there with his mouth open, lost for words. Finally he said, "Dr. Williams, I can't give you fifteen acres of land." I informed him, "It's your land; you can do with it as you please." As the color returned to his face and he regrouped, the president said, "Wait a minute; I'll be right back." He left the room and returned a few minutes later. "Now this is the deal," he said. "We'll let you have the fifteen acres for $12,000 and we'll finance it for you." Now, if you know anything about real estate and purchasing land, with that price he did give it to us!

We returned to the church shouting and praising God for how He had, once again, come to our rescue. Our faith in Him had brought us to another milestone we could record in the history of this ministry. We know that faith without works is dead. God is saying, "Give Me something to work with." Faith is the confident assurance that what we hope for is going to happen. It is the evidence of things we cannot yet see. God rewards those who sincerely seek Him. When you ask God, be sure that you really expect Him to answer, for a doubtful mind is as unsettled as a wave of the sea that is driven and tossed by the wind. Individuals like that should not expect to receive anything from the Lord.

Faith: belief or trust, especially in a higher power. The fundamental idea in Scripture is steadfastness and faithfulness. Faith is a quality highly prized in Scripture. Hebrews 11:6 sums this up by saying that "without faith it is impossible to please God." The word is used in Scripture (1) most frequently in a subjective sense, denoting a moral and spiritual quality of individuals, by virtue of which men are held in relations of confidence in God and fidelity to Him; (2) in an objective sense, meaning the body of truth, moral and religious, which God has revealed of that which men believe.

Philosophical: Faith, viewed philosophically, must be regarded as lying at the basis of all knowledge. Anselm's famous utterance *"Crede ut intelligas"* ("Believe that you may know") expresses the truth in contrast with the words of Abelard, *"Intellige ut credas"* ("Know that you may believe"). Truths perceived intuitively imply faith in the intuitions. Truths or facts arrived at by logical processes, or processes of reasoning, are held to be known because, first of all, we have confidence in the laws of the human mind. Our knowledge obtained through the senses has underneath it faith in the senses. A large part of knowledge rests upon human testimony, and of course this involves faith in the testimony.

Theological: Faith in the theological sense contains two elements recognized in the Scriptures: there is an element that is intellectual and also an element, of even deeper importance that is moral. Faith is not simply the assent of the intellect to revealed truth; it is the practical submission of the entire man to the guidance and control of such truth. "The devils also believe, and tremble" (James 2:19).

The various synonyms of the Bible for *faith* help to illustrate its nature and action:

Hear—"Faith cometh by hearing." (Romans 10:17); "Hear, and your soul shall live." (Isaiah 55:3)

Look—"Look unto me and be ye saved." (Isaiah 45:22)

The listening soul looks out and waits until God is revealed. Looking, *He* becomes real, and then *His Word* and *His deliverance* becomes real.

Receive: "But as many as received him, to them gave he power to become the sons of God, even to them that believe on his name" (John 1:12). Faith is the hand receiving and appropriating the divine gift, and grasping all of God's treasures. Even when all is dark, faith does not tremble, seeing the everlasting hand of our omnipotent God, he holds the frail hand outstretched to Him.

Believe: The word translated *believe* is found 247 times in the New Testament, and the kindred term *faith* occurs 244 times, while *faithful*, which simply means "full of faith" appears 67 times. The Greek word for *believe* means "to persuade, to give credit to, to trust or confide in." The Hebrew word for *believe* means "to stay, to support, and then, that which forms the stay, its foundation." It is from the Hebrew word that derives the English term *amen*, signifying "of a truth," or "so be it." So when we read that Abraham believed God, he actually "amen" Him.

All through the New Testament, we find "faith" referred to as attending every step of Christian experience, from its commencement to its consummation. At all times and under all circumstances, such faith is essential.

"He that believeth and is baptized shall be saved; but he that believeth not shall be damned." (Mark 16:16)

"For whatsoever is not of faith is sin." (Romans 14:23)

"So we see that they could not enter in because of unbelief."(Hebrews 3:19)

Spelled out as an acrostic, faith means:

> **F**orsaking
> **A**ll
> **I**
> **T**rust
> **H**im

This faith we are considering is not a blind, unintelligent act of the mind, nor is it credulity. It rests upon knowledge of God as revealed in His Word. Ours is not a blind trust in an unknown stranger: "They that know Thy name will put their trust in Thee" (Psalm 9:10). Faith through knowledge leads to commitment. It reaches its end in surrender. "According to the glorious gospel of the blessed God, which was committed to my trust" (1 Timothy 1:11). A person may know that a bank is sound and trusts its security, but only when a transfer of funds has taken place has actual business been done.

Chapter 6
Doubt: It's a Trap

> Our doubts are traitors and make us lose the good we
> oft might win, by fearing to attempt.
> —William Shakespeare

A trap is a device designed to catch an animal and kill it or prevent it from escaping, e.g., a concealed pit or a mechanical device that springs shut. Looking at a trap from a confining situation, it is a situation from which it is difficult to escape and in which somebody feels confined, restricted, or in somebody else's power.

The doubt trap is when you imprison yourself, or when you are caught in the trap of your own feeling of uncertainties, insecurities, and a lack of conviction which is only surpassed by fear. As Mr. William James has so ingenuously stated, "If you believe that feeling bad or worrying long enough will change a past or future event, then you are residing on another planet with a different reality system." It is a proven fact that when you doubt your power, you give power to your doubt.

What Is Doubt?

Remember *pistis* is "belief, being persuaded, having confidence." So the opposite of confidence, is doubt. Doubt is a hindrance because it also has true existence—it is a true obstacle in the spirit. It actually exists as a weight in the spirit, and caused Peter to begin sinking after walking on water! Doubt means "to separate, make a distinction, to withdraw, oppose, strive with dispute, contend, be at variance with one's self, and hesitate." The existence of doubt causes you to be void of peace, to have a sinking in your spirit—it is a striving *against* what you are trying to obtain. Doubt is a feeling of uncertainty or lack of conviction. Doubt is the status between belief and disbelief, involves uncertainty or distrust or lack of sureness of an alleged fact, an action, a motive, or a decision. It causes both anxiety and apprehension. Doubt is active fear. It our inability to see events and actions as anything else but negative. It causes us to rely on our best thinking to interpret events and actions, but if we are predisposed to seeing them as dangerous, it is nearly impossible to see them any other way.

The world is full of threats. But we can turn adversity into opportunity by remaining calm and allowing the events to play out, rather than to react and find we made things worse. Doubt in our own abilities or the abilities of others, in the loyalty of another, in their sincerity, their love, their fidelity, sets into motion reactions that could have been avoided altogether, had we only reacted a different way. It was not the truth that caused the problem; it was the doubt that exacerbated the fear.

Doubt can only be managed by having strong values and principles. But knowing what you believe to be true at its core, is true. And you must cling to that truth through the storms. It is the lack of these anchors that causes one to doubt their own abilities, coping skills, and analytical tools. If the world is a cube, all the self-confidence is worthless. But with principles and tools that can assess information and see beyond what is to what might be, doubt can disappear.

As a Christian, truth for me is the Bible. It is the foundation of my values and beliefs. If I cling to those through the storms, doubt cannot dissuade me. But if I let them go and start to cling to my abilities and skills, to cling to the things of this world, then I am casting about for stability which is not there. The only rock is biblical truth. Doubt can also be defined as following:

1. To be undecided or skeptical about: begin to doubt some accepted doctrines
2. To tend to disbelieve; distrust: doubts politicians when they make sweeping statements
3. To regard as unlikely: I doubt that we'll arrive on time
4. Archaic: to suspect; fear
5. A lack of certainty that often leads to irresolution

THE POWER OF YOUR FAITH

6. A lack of trust
7. A point about which one is uncertain or skeptical: reassured me by answering my doubts
8. The condition of being unsettled or unresolved: an outcome still in doubt

Now that we have been enlightened on what doubt, fear, and worrying is, let's look into how to rid ourselves of it.

Worry, doubt, and fear are to be dreaded more than the plague when you're on the path of self-actualization, to becoming who you truly are. It's insidious, creeping up on you slowly and inevitably from the moment you ask yourself the first doubting questions "Can I really do this?" "What did I get myself into?" "I must have been crazy to think that." These mental exclamations hide a significant truth. You're nervous and afraid to succeed. That opens a breach in your foundation through which fear enters. It is felt immediately and you tell yourself to "be positive," which is nonsensical. The problem lies in your lack of self-confidence because suddenly, you don't feel capable.

Because feelings progress to thoughts, words, and finally to action, you relive thoughts of past experiences which inundate you and underscore your self-doubt. It's because you lost focus. And as a result, you feel lost, misplace stuff, forget what you were doing, maybe have near-misses when you're driving; these incidents cause you to criticize yourself more.

We have all been there. I certainly have, which is how this book was born. We all go through these phases. What's important is the lesson you learn from a particular experience. Get rid of the worry, doubt, and fear; they are the sources of harm to success in any endeavor. Becoming self-aware is your only choice.

You Need To:

1. **Be compassionate with yourself.** Yes, be nice to yourself; stop beating yourself up!
2. **Understand what triggered the first thought** which led to your temporary breakdown into despair, and why. Those "what ifs" are not new. It's time to unmask the culprit.
3. **Take ten long, slow, deep breaths to calm down.** Oxygenate

your brain. Then take ten more and ten more after that if necessary, until you feel calm and your shoulders and/or stomach relax.

4. **Start a personal journal.** Write down *what* you feel physically (stiff shoulders, tense stomach, etc.); *how* you feel emotionally (crappy and stressed are *not* emotions; sad, nervous, anxious, afraid, etc., are); and *why*. The more you externalize your feelings, the calmer, more focused and relaxed you will feel.

5. **Start a success journal.** Jack Canfield advises you to write down your daily goals and complete them every evening by also writing down what you accomplished. No matter how small. It's your pat on the back, so write it down. Take the time to record every success in your life which you can remember. Writing down your accomplishments (a) records them in your subconscious mind, and (b) makes you feel good. Reread them to keep you in a positive frame of mind.

6. **Start a gratitude journal.** Write down every morning and/or evening five things for which you're grateful. Every little thing helps when times are hard. Positivity breeds positivity.

7. **Every day reread your goals** and the plans you made to take you there. Reaffirming your purpose is essential—it keeps you on track.

8. **Meditate for twenty to thirty minutes every day.** Either first thing in the morning to jump-start your day or in the evening to decompress. Find a relaxation method that works for you. A calm center is necessary because when "stuff" happens that's when you will need it most.

These methods are meant to illustrate how becoming self-aware could benefit you. It is in your best interests to rid yourself of worry, doubt, and fear if you want to live a long and healthy life. When you become self-aware, you are able to take back your power and create the life you want for yourself. You are now empowered to stop worrying.

Mr. Dale Carnegie also gives us excellent advice. This is part of his 1948 book summary on *How to Stop Worrying and Start Living*.

Seven ways to cultivate a mental attitude that will bring you peace and happiness.

1. Let's fill our minds with thoughts of peace, courage, health, and hope, for "our life is what our thoughts make it."
2. Let's never try to get even with our enemies, because if we do we will hurt ourselves far more than we hurt them. Do as General Eisenhower did: never waste a minute thinking about people we don't like.
3. Instead of worrying about ingratitude, let's expect it. Let's remember that Jesus healed ten lepers in one day—and only one thanked Him. Why should we expect more gratitude than Jesus got?
   A. Let's remember that the only way to find happiness is not to expect gratitude—but to give for the joy of giving.
   B. Let's remember that gratitude is a "cultivated" trait; so if we want our children to be grateful, we must train them to be grateful.
4. Count your blessings—not your troubles!
5. Let's not imitate others. Let's find ourselves and be ourselves, for "envy is ignorance" and "imitation is suicide."
6. When fate hands us a lemon, let's try to make lemonade.
7. Let's forget our own unhappiness—by trying to create a little happiness for others. *When you are good to others, you are best to yourself* (emphasis added).

Putting this advice into practice will develop a new way of thinking because the worry habit is a killer. Let's stop worrying and start praising the Lord. It has been my experience that you block your dream when you allow fear and doubt to grow bigger than your faith.

Chapter 7
The Importance of Faith

Faith is a quality highly prized in Scripture. Hebrews 11:6 sums this up by saying that "without faith it is impossible to please God." There are various aspects and degrees of faith that are the clear teaching Paul emphasizes when he speaks of faith leading to more faith: "For therein is the righteousness of God revealed from faith to faith: as it is written, the just shall live by faith" (Romans 1:17). But whatever degree of faith we have, Christ is the author of it all.

> Looking unto Jesus the author and finisher of our faith; who for the joy that was set before him endured the cross, despising the shame, and is set down at the right hand of the throne of God.
>
> (Hebrews 12:2)

The quality of one's life is directly linked to the quality of faith one presents. That's the reason why many believers live a life without quality. They pray, attend church meetings, and follow God's Word in their own way; but when it comes to acting out their faith according to God's teachings, they simply decline.

When the subject is faith with quality, the name that first comes to mind is Abraham, because when called by God, he left country, family, and his father's house and followed God's voice. Why? Because of his faith. He believed God's promise, and his faith was materialized through his actions. It took him twenty-five years to see the main promise fulfilled, which was to have a son with his wife, Sarah; however, during these years, he never gave up following God's Word and kept being blessed every step of the way.

By the time Isaac was born, God had already made Abraham great, and covered him with wealth and honor. And when tested, Abraham once again followed the voice of faith, not denying God what He asked of him, which was his lifetime dream on the altar on Mount Moriah. Once again Abraham proved beyond any doubt the quality of his faith. Because of what he did, God made an oath that He would surely bless Abraham and his descendants, and He indeed blessed him. This blessing still stands today!

How much faith do I need to activate, to move my situation? Do I need a mountain-size faith to move mountain or do I need a mulberry tree–size faith to move a mulberry tree (see Luke 17:5–6)? In other words, does my faith have to be in direct proportion to the size of my challenge? The answer is no. Jesus states: "If you had faith the size of a mustard seed, you could say to this mulberry tree, 'Be uprooted and planted in the sea,' and it would obey you." He makes reference to a mustard seed which is one of the smallest seeds there is to show how insignificant the amount of faith needed. It's not the quantity of your faith; it's the quality. Faith believes in divine possibilities. This is to say faith is allowing the possibility that God can intervene in our situation at any given time.

There is another remarkable incident in the life of Jesus. This time the hero is a Roman centurion. The response of the centurion made Jesus exclaim, "I have not found so great faith, no, not in Israel" (Matthew 8:10). What is the type of faith that the centurion had? He had faith without doubt. It was a clean faith, no fizzy bubbly faith. He had known from experience that if an officer commands, that is done. He believed that Jesus was greater than himself and Jesus's words did have power to heal his servant. He had absolutely no doubt that Jesus could heal his servant. He had faith in Jesus that by His word alone, He could heal. That is why he did not bother to carry his servant to the presence of Jesus.

When we pray to God, we always make sure we know where the fire exit is. When we entrust our matters to Jesus, we often make sure the lifeboat is serviced and ready or the parachute works properly. In case God fails, we have some alternative to escape! This sort of faith with bubbles of doubt cannot achieve anything. We disappoint God when we offer our cup of faith to God, because God looks at the faith and not the bubbles, so he knows that it is only half full. Let us not pray to increase our faith but ask God to help us to cultivate quality faith. This faith, Jesus says, can do great things: it can even move mountains.

The Bible concordance reveals these degrees of faith. Where does experience place us?

No Faith

> And he said, I will hide my face from them, I will see what their end shall be: for they are a forward generation, children in whom is no faith.
>
> (Deuteronomy 32:20)

> And he said unto then, why are ye so fearful? how is it that ye have no faith?
>
> (Mark 4:40)

In both cases those addressed belonged to God, yet were destitute of a Spirit-inspired faith in divine ability to meet the crisis of the hour. While faith mentioned in these references is wholehearted trust and confidence in God, "faith" is used to describe the body of revealed doctrine. Our Lord asked whether He would find "the faith" that is, the sum of truth as found in the Scriptures, when He returns. "I tell you that he will avenge them speedily. Nevertheless when the Son of man cometh, shall he find faith on the earth?" (Luke 18:8).

Little Faith

> O ye of little faith.
>
> (Matthew 8:26)

> O ye of little faith, wherefore didst thou doubt.
>
> (Matthew 14:31)

It is evident from the question of the Lord that little faith is equivalent to lack of faith. Faith, although "little," can be effective if it is directed toward the Lord. If the quantity of faith is small, it can be increased. If the quality of faith is of the wrong sort, it can be purged and directed into the right channel.

Weak Faith

> Him that is weak in the faith, receive ye.
> (Romans 14:1)

The context implies the observance of liberty when it comes to matters not expressly forbidden in Scripture. Tolerance is necessary when we encounter those who are weak in the faith, that is, who do not have full spiritual intuition and guidance. Abraham was not weak in faith, but strong in such a virtue (Romans 4:19–20).

Dead Faith

> Faith, if it hath not works, is dead, being alone.
> (James 2:17)

Faith in God should become active in service for God. Works cannot save, but they are the evidence of salvation. Living faith is that which obeys, serves, and suffers. We have many in the church that have faith, but it is not the kind that leads one to action. Our knowledge of the God's Word needs to be put into practice so that our faith becomes a living faith. If we do not put God's Word into practice, our faith will become weaker and weaker, and eventually become a dead faith and collapse.

Great Faith

> I have not found so great faith, no, not in Israel.
> (Luke 7:9)

Jesus commended the centurion for his remarkable faith, and at the same time rebuked the religious leaders for their lack of trust in Him. The Gentile soldier had a spiritual discernment of Christ's authority and power, but the leaders in Israel lacked it.

Full of Faith

> Barnabas was full of the Holy Ghost and of faith.
>
> (Acts 11:24)

Barnabas was full of faith because he was full of the Spirit. How much faith is an individual capable of? We cannot say. When you are full to capacity, God enlarges the capacity. This is evident: if one is full of faith, there is no room for doubt, mistrust, or despair.

Steadfast Faith

> The steadfastness of your faith in Christ.
>
> (Colossians 2:5)

If faith is to be steadfast, meaning rooted and grounded so that winds of doubt or trial never will move it, it must be "in Christ." It is by this steadfast faith that we can resist the devil (1 Peter 5:9). Such a strong, steadfast faith will be tested, but it will abide the fiery trial (1 Peter 1:7). This is the kind of faith the saints are to exhibit during great trials and tribulation.

Unfeigned Faith

> Faith unfeigned.
>
> (2 Timothy 1:5)

The word *unfeigned* means "without counterfeit or hypocrisy." The faith Paul commended was sincere and genuine. There was nothing false about it.

Holy Faith

> Building up yourselves on your most holy faith.
>
> (Jude 20)

Such a faith is rightly called a "holy faith," because it is with the Holy Son. It is also a holy faith because it results in a holy life. Having laid our foundation well in a sound faith, we must build upon it; and we should take care with what materials we carry on our building. Right principles will stand the test even on the fiery trial.

Chapter 8
Enemies of Faith

Fight the good fight of faith, lay hold on eternal life, whereunto thou art also called, and hast professed a good profession before many witnesses.

(1 Timothy 6:12)

I n this chapter we are going to deal with some hindrances to faith. There wouldn't be a fight if there were no enemies of faith. But the enemies of faith are not what people think they are. Most people look for enemies in the natural realm, and that's not where they are at all. This is a spiritual warfare: "For the weapons of our warfare are not carnal, but mighty through God to the pulling down of strong holds" (2 Corinthians 10:4).

The Bible says in Romans 10:17, "So then faith cometh by hearing, and hearing the word of God." *The greatest hindrance to faith is a lack of knowledge of God's Word.* Because faith comes by hearing the Word of God, all the enemies of faith will be connected in some way with our lack of knowledge of God's Word.

If you have knowledge of God's Word, nothing can keep it from working, because it comes by hearing. If you have heard the Word, you have faith. People pray to get faith, yet faith only comes by hearing the Word of God. If you could get it by praying for it, then Romans 10:17 would be untrue. People who pray for faith are attempting to get what the Word alone can give.

One of the most prominent enemies of faith is a *sense of unworthiness.* All of us have had a battle with that. A sense of unworthiness and a sense of lack of faith go hand in hand. These two are perhaps the most subtle, dangerous weapons of the devil.

We can find the answer to these feelings in God's Word. The answer is this: Your worthiness is Jesus Christ! God does not heal your body or baptize you in the Holy Spirit on the basis of your individual worthiness. If He did, no one would ever receive these blessings from God, because no man could be worthy in his or her own right.

Not knowing the Word, many Christians allow feelings of unworthiness to defeat them. I have heard it more times than I care to remember of people feeling they would not receive the Holy Spirit because they were not good enough—they were unworthy.

The trouble is that the individual looks at himself from the natural standpoint. He is acquainted with all of his shortcomings, mistakes, faults, and failures, and he looks at himself from a natural standpoint rather than from the biblical standpoint—the way God looks at him. Many of us struggle with the same thing, especially in our youth; we are weak and unworthy from the natural standpoint but not from a biblical perspective.

The Bible says, "The entrance of thy words giveth light" (Psalm 119:130), and once the light is in your spirit, it can't be removed, even though the devil will do his best to confuse you. He will always try to keep you from walking in the light so you will remain in darkness—the darkness in regard to God's Word. You will remain in your condition until you come to yourself and begin walking in the Word of God.

Second Corinthians 5:17 says, "Therefore if any man be in Christ, he is a new creature: old things are passed away; behold all things are become new." Paul said, writing to the church at Ephesus, "For we are his workmanship, created in Christ Jesus unto good works, which God hath before ordained that we should walk in them" (Ephesians 2:10). We did not make ourselves new creatures; He made us new creatures. Ephesians 4:24 continues, "And that ye put on the new man, which after God is created in righteousness and true holiness."

Ask yourself, does God make unworthy new creatures? Would He make a new creature that wasn't good enough to stand in His presence? The mistake that is made is that instead of believing what the Bible says about you—the real you, the man on the inside—you are looking at the outward man and his physical shortcomings. We pass judgment on ourselves instead of accepting God's estimation of it. God does not make unworthy creatures. If He did, what does that said about His work?

He made us a new creature in Christ Jesus. Our worthiness is Christ Jesus. I look a lot better in Him than I do any other way! And that is the way God sees me: in Him. He doesn't really see me; He looks at Jesus and sees me in Jesus, as Paul stated: "Therefore if any man be *in Christ*, he is a new creature: old things are passed away; behold, all things are become new" (emphasis added).

The Word of God will help you rid yourself of this sense of unworthiness; and when you are rid of it, the sense of the lack of faith also will leave. They are tormenting twins of the enemy that have come to rob you of the blessings Christ secured for you.

Another enemy of faith—the reason so many are defeated in their faith life—is that they accept *a substitute for faith*. They try to substitute either hope or mental agreement for faith.

Often, you can hear individuals say, "Well, I'm hoping and praying ..." There are times when we make the statement as we depart on our journey: "I hope and pray you will have a safe trip." That prayer is in vain because it is in hope. Nowhere in the Bible does it say that God hears the prayer of hope. The Bible speaks of the prayer of faith: "And the prayer of faith shall save the sick" (James 5:15). If James had said the prayer of hope would do it, we would all automatically have results, because hope is the natural human thing to do. Jesus taught, "What things soever ye desire, when ye pray, *believe* that ye receive them, and ye shall have them" (Mark 11:24, emphasis added). Believe—not hope—that you receive.

Faith is present tense. "Now faith is the substance of things hoped for, the evidence of things not seen." *I'm not wishing it will happen; I'm expecting it to happen!* Hope doesn't have any substance, but faith gives substance to what you hope for. It is your faith that gives substance to the healing in your life. It is there in the spirit realm, but you want it here in this substance realm where it can be seen and felt. Your faith gives substance to that.

From Brother Kenneth Hagin from Real Faith: A marvelous example of real faith that stands on God's Word in the face of all apparent contradictions was the healing of a certain nine-year-old boy.

Three doctors—two were specialists—had given him up to die. They said, "We've done all we can. There isn't a thing that can be done medically. The boy's kidneys have stopped functioning. It is just a matter of time and he will be gone." When neither of the child's parents spoke or showed any sign of emotion, the doctor, thinking they were too shocked to speak, repeated what he had just said and concluded with the statement, "Your child will be dead shortly."

"No, doctor," they said calmly. "He will not die. The Word of God says in Matthew 8:17, 'Himself took our infirmities and bare our sicknesses.' Our child will live."

The child was in intensive care. His mother could go in to see him for ten minutes in the morning, and his father could see him briefly at night. The father told the boy, "Now, Son, if you don't sleep, quote the Scripture in Matthew 8:17 all night long and say, 'Himself took my infirmities and bare my sicknesses. Himself took my infirmities and bare my sicknesses. Himself took my infirmities and bare my sicknesses. By His stripes I am healed.'" After three nights of repeating that, the boy was healed and went home.

When the crisis came, these parents were prepared for it. They were well fortified with the Word of God. Faith cometh by hearing, hearing by the Word of God. Their believing was in the right place: not in what their physical sense told them—not in the circumstances surrounding them—but in what God's Word said.

Another enemy of faith is wavering.

James 1:6–7 warns, "But let him ask in faith, nothing wavering. For he that wavereth is like a wave of the sea driven with the wind and tossed. For let not that man (the one who wavers) think that he shall receive any thing of the Lord."

Our faith wavers when:

> We apply human thinking to our circumstances. Sometimes God is going to require us to do something with which human reasoning disagrees (Isaiah 55:9).

> We allow our feelings to overcome our faith. It could be a sense of unworthiness or inadequacy that trips us

up. Fear of criticism or failure might cause us to doubt we can do what He asks.

We fail to see God at work in our circumstances. Doubts creep in when we have asked Him to take action but nothing appears to be happening.

We have guilt over sin, past or present. We cannot operate with strong faith when we are under conviction of sin or dwelling on guilt over past wrongdoing.

We listen to the enemy's lies. Satan is the father of lies, whose objective is to have us reject God's truth and believe his deception instead.

Faith is defined as "being sure of what we hope for and certain of what we do not see" (Hebrews 11:1 NIV).

Although healing is manifested in the physical realm, it actually is a spiritual blessing because it is spiritual healing. God is not going to heal your body. He is not going to do one thing about healing you. He's already done all He is ever going to do about healing you, because He laid your sickness and disease on Jesus. Jesus already has borne them for you, and by His stripes "ye were healed."

Get your believing in line with what the Word of God says. Quit hoping. Start believing that by His stripes you are healed—not because you feel like it or see it, but because His Word says it. Start saying, "According to His Word, I am healed." If you are asked how you do feel, answer according to the Word, not according to the natural. We walk by faith, not by sight.

Fear: The Enemy of Your Faith

Faith and fear are opposites but work the same way. God will do nothing without faith and the devil can do nothing without fear. These two work the same way.

What is fear keeping you from doing today? Is there something that you are aspiring to accomplish, but you are allowing fear to hold you back? Fear interrupts your ability to operate in faith. Fear is the twin of doubt and the enemy to your faith. Fear and doubt keep you from walking in faith. It is a negative cycle that prevents you from receiving answered prayers and robs you of an abundant life. "Faith is the confidence that what we hope for will actually happen; it gives us assurance about things we cannot see" (Hebrews 11:1 NLT).

Many times our prayers go unanswered because we have allowed fear to enter into our hearts. You cannot have both fear and faith operating at the same time. That is called being doubled-minded. A double-minded man should not expect to receive anything from God, according to the Bible (James 1:7 KJV). You are either walking in faith or in fear. Sometimes we think it is noble to worry about something, otherwise we seem careless (what does this mean?). To the contrary, fear is an enemy that traps people in and keeps them from seeing the wonderful working power of God in their lives.

I love what the Amplified Bible says in 2 Timothy 1:7: "For God did not give us a spirit of timidity (of cowardice, of craven and cringing and fawning fear), but [He has given us a spirit] of power and of love and of calm and well-balanced mind." You have to understand the fact that fear did not originate from God. We know that God is love. Therefore, He does not have fear to give.

Fear will prevent you from enjoying the good life. Many people are paralyzed from moving forward in different areas because of fear. It could be fear of relationships, stepping out into new territory, fear of confrontation, fear of illness, or fear of not having enough—the list can go on and on. Have you ever read the story of Job? Talk about tragedy! Job recognized early on that his fears caused some of the negative outcomes in his life. He said, "What I always feared has happened to me. What I dreaded has come true" (Job 3:25 NLT).

Fear, the enemy of faith, has no victory in your life when you make a decision to walk in faith. "Nothing is impossible with God" (Luke 1:37 KJV).

> You block your dream when you allow your fear to grow bigger than your faith.
>
> —Mary Manin Morrissey

I truly believe that all our fears hinge on failing; we are very concerned of what others will think of us. Consequently we unconsciously become men-pleasers rather than God-pleasers. To be successful, how must we overcome the fear of failure?

Overcoming the Fear of Failure

Fear of failure is one of the greatest fears people have. It is closely related to fear of criticism and fear of rejection. Successful people overcome their fear of failure. Fear incapacitates unsuccessful people.

The law of feedback states: there is no failure; there is only feedback. Successful people look at mistakes as outcomes or results, not as failure. Unsuccessful people look at mistakes as permanent and personal. Buckminster Fuller wrote, "Whatever humans have learned had to be learned as a consequence only of trial-and-error experience. Humans have learned only through mistakes."

Most people self-limit themselves. Most people do not achieve a fraction of what they are capable of achieving, because they are afraid to try and fail. Take these steps to overcome your fear of failure and move yourself forward to getting the result you desire:

Step One: Take action. Bold, decisive action. Do something scary. Fear of failure immobilizes you. To overcome this fear, you must act. When you act, act boldly. Action gives you the power to change the circumstances or the situation. You must overcome the inertia by doing something. Dr. Robert Schuller asks, "What would you do if you knew you could not fail?" What could you achieve? Be brave and just do it. If it doesn't work out the way you want, then do something else. But *do something now.*

Step Two: Persist. Successful people just don't give up. They keep trying different approaches to achieving their outcomes until they finally get the results they want. Unsuccessful people try one thing that doesn't work and then give up. Often people give up when they are on the threshold of succeeding.

Step Three: Don't take failure personally. Failure is about behavior, outcomes, and results. Failure is not a personality characteristic. Although what you do may not give you the result you wanted, it doesn't mean you are a failure. Because you made a mistake, doesn't mean that you are a failure.

Step Four: Do things differently. If what you are doing isn't working, do something else. There is an old saying: If you always do what you've always done, you'll always get what you always got. If you're not getting the results you want, then you must do something different. Most people stop doing anything at all, and this guarantees they won't be successful.

Step Five: Don't be so hard on yourself. Hey, if nothing else, you know what doesn't work. Failure is a judgment or evaluation of behavior. Look at failure as an event or a happening, not as a person.

Step Six: Treat the experience as an opportunity to learn. Think of failure as a learning experience. What did you learn from the experience that will help you in the future? How can you use the experience to improve yourself or your situation? Ask yourself these questions:

1. What was the mistake?
2. Why did it happen?
3. How could it have been prevented?
4. How can I do better next time?

Then use what you learned from the experience to do things differently so you get different results next time. Learn from the experience or ignore it.

Step Seven: Look for possible opportunities that result from the experience. Napoleon Hill, author of *Think and Grow Rich*, says "every adversity, every failure and every heartache carries with it the seed of an equivalent or a greater benefit." Look for the opportunity and the benefit.

Step Eight: Fail forward fast. Tom Peters, the management guru, says that in today's business world, companies must fail forward fast. What he means is that the way we learn is by making mistakes. So if we want to learn at a faster pace, we must make mistakes at a faster pace. The key is that you must learn from the mistakes you make so you don't repeat them.

Although we all make mistakes, fear of failure doesn't have to cripple you. As self-help author Susan Jeffers says, *"Feel the fear and do it anyway."*

Chapter 9
How to Keep Faith in Tough Times

In these tough times, we must apply faith and hope in the promises God has made to those who believe, obey and trust in Him. Norman Vincent Peale said, "Tough times don't last but tough people do. You have got to toughen up or you will melt away in this pot of boiling discouraging news."

I know that sometimes it is difficult to be strong in faith when things around us and circumstances in our lives seem so gloomy. For those of us who believe in Christ, there is always hope and trust that in our darkest moments, God's light still shines through. When you feel as though you are at the end of the rope, do not let go. Hold tighter; the longer you hold on, the greater your blessings will be. Remember, "Nothing that is worthwhile comes without a struggle," and "Nothing is too hard for the Lord," and "With God all things are possible"—not some things, *all things*.

In Mark 12:41–44 Jesus gives us an example of belief that isn't determined by circumstance. In this story a widow who is poverty stricken presents two copper mites (the equivalent of half a cent) as her offering, and Jesus points out to His disciples that she has contributed the most to the treasury because she has put in everything she has. Here was a penniless widow, without a future source of income and no one to care for her, and in the depth of her desperation her faith cried out to God. Some would have mocked her and mocked God through her. "The God of your lack," they might have taunted. But in her circumstance, she said to God that her faith remained in Him.

Second Kings 4:1–7 tells the story of a widow whose two sons would be enslaved if she was unable to pay off her late husband's debt. Her story is reflective of the challenges being faced by many of us today, who like her find ourselves in difficult situations due to no fault of our own. Many have served faithfully in their sectors of employment and yet have been let go, or their employers were forced to close shop, and even for others who have managed to retain their jobs, the cost of everyday life has become a major challenge.

When the widow presented her situation to Elisha, he asked her to tell him what she had in her house. She replied that she had a little oil, and he instructed her to go round to her neighbors to ask for all the empty jars they could provide. He asked her to pour her oil into the jars, and the little she had kept flowing until there wasn't an empty jar left. What this miracle showed was that opportunities existed even in the midst of her suffering. In the same way, many of us will find endless opportunities in this credit crunch if we remain tuned into the voice of God.

Isaac was tuned into the voice of God in Genesis 26 and despite a famine in the land, verse 12 records that he "planted crops in that land and the same year reaped a hundredfold, because the LORD blessed him." Prior to this prosperity, God had instructed him not to go down to Egypt—as the Israelites often did in times of famine—but to dwell in a land He would tell him about, so Isaac was able to thrive in adverse conditions.

Similar opportunities exist for those affected by the credit crunch, and many of us will find ourselves challenged more than ever to step out in faith in these troubled times. I would like to encourage you, if you fall into that category, to put your complete trust in God at this time, knowing that He is able to supply all your needs. The widow of the prophet multiplied what little she had, and at the end of her story, she was able to pay off her debts and also to provide for her family's needs.

With the knowledge that God is always with you, put on your tough skin and know that the battle is already won.

Apply These Principles

1. Read the Bible often, listen to what it is saying to you and act accordingly.

    So then faith, cometh by hearing, and hearing by the word of God.

    (Romans 10:17)

2. Have faith, do not doubt. Believe in God and work earnestly on developing the measure of faith that He has given you.

God hath dealt to every man the measure of faith.

(Romans 12:3)

3. Walk by faith and not by sight. Do not be too concerned about the hardships, unpleasant experiences, or frustration that you encounter in the natural realm of things. The supernatural realm is always working favorably for you, even in the midst of the chaos you see.

For we walk by faith, not by sight.

(2 Corinthians 5:7)

4. Believe in yourself. You have sufficient faith. Use it.

I tell you the truth, if you have faith as small as a mustard seed, you can say to this mountain, "Move from here to there" and it will move. Nothing will be impossible for you.

(Matthew 17:20)

5. Pray often. Prayer is the key.

Pray without ceasing

(1 Thessalonians 5:17)

Beliefnet give us ten tips in recharging our faith life:

1. Look behind

If God or any divine energy seems far away, take a moment to remember a time when you had God's help in the past. Was it a time of family trouble? Illness? Job loss? A moment when you felt an internal nudge to call a friend—and it turned out she needed to hear from you?

When you remember times of divine guidance in the past, you can develop gratitude and look for divine guidance in the present.

2. Take a time out

If a time-out works for children, it can work for you. It's not about punishing yourself, it's about pulling away from all the daily distractions, the frustrations, and the tantrum-inducing surroundings you deal with every day.

If you can get away to a relaxing pond, do it. If that's not an option, a few quiet moments to breathe and to be grateful can restore your equilibrium.

3. Visit a house of worship

Okay, okay, so the last time you went to church/synagogue/mosque or temple, the spiritual leader was boring/offensive/caught up in a scandal. Don't let someone else's flaws derail your spiritual journey.

Try another house of worship. Remember that you can find divine inspiration in the Scripture readings, the hymns, and the chats with congregation members after services.

4. Hit the bookstore

Every day someone is writing a new inspirational book or a new guide to prayer. You don't have to read all of them or even like them.

Just keep an eye out for something that speaks to you—even if the theme is something like, "How to feel closer to God when you just want to take a nap."

5. Don't run from doubt

Sometimes that "blah" feeling can mask major doubts. Doubts can feel scary, but if you're wrestling with deep questions of faith, that's okay. You're not the first (just check out the biblical book of Job.)

If you have questions, look for answers. Just as exercise strengthens your muscles, the process of searching may strengthen your faith, and chances are you'll discover at least a few helpful hints along the way.

6. Read Scriptures

Each faith has its holy books, the places where believers have looked again and again for inspiration, hope, and guidance. These books will have something that speaks to you.

Even if you find answers elsewhere, reading about the struggles that faced the founders of your faith is bound to nurture your own faith journey.

7. Pray or meditate

You don't have to pray like a saint or meditate like a guru. Just stop running and chattering long enough to breathe.

If you feel too uninspired to come up with your own prayer, take a look at the prayers or meditations from your faith tradition. You may find that someone centuries ago wrote words that give voice to what you're feeling today.

8. Talk to someone

Even Mother Teresa had times when she didn't feel God's presence. (And let's face it, most of us are no Mother Teresa.) Don't bury your doubts and frustrations. Find a friend who'll listen respectfully.

It's probably best not to choose someone who will make fun of you for believing in anything other than a spreadsheet or someone who's going to call you a heretic for asking a question. The simple act of telling someone how you feel may take away a bit of the burden.

9. Practice gratitude

It's hard to be grateful when everything seems the same as it ever was. There's no need to deny your feelings, but it's also important to appreciate the good stuff. Start by making a mental list. Write it down and carry it in your wallet for reference.

So where do you start? No surprise—it's with the small stuff like a good cup of coffee. A good morning commute. A friend/sibling/spouse/pet that makes you laugh, at least once in a while.

10. Wait for high tide

Sometimes your faith life just feels like a tidal pool, a bit shallow or still, no matter what you do. Remember high tide will come, and soon you'll be back in the deep water. Just as the seasons change, this season of your faith life will end.

During these times, the most important thing is to keep going, to have enough faith to get to the next day, and to keep your eyes open for something beautiful and surprising. One of these days, the tide is bound to turn.

Chapter 10
Rise Up and Stand Tall!

When you sit or recline in a comfortable chair or on the couch—perhaps looking at the television—you can feel the pull of inertia to stay where you are, rather than getting up and moving around. That's obvious, but what isn't so obvious is why would anyone want to put themselves in that position for long periods of time. As soon as you settle in, it's an invitation to munch on something—usually the wrong foods. The same hold true when you allow negative thoughts to "settle in"—you have just given ammunition to the devil to fight you. Faith is an *action* word; if you want it to work for you, you must work it! Stand tall and keep walking by faith.

> But the boat was by this time out on the sea, many furlongs (a furlong is one-eight of a mile) distant from the land, beaten and tossed by the waves, for the wind was against them. And in the fourth watch (between 3:00–6:00 a.m.) of the night, Jesus came to them, walking on the sea. And when the disciples saw Him walking on the sea, they were terrified and said, It is a ghost! And they screamed out with fright.

> But instantly He spoke to them, saying, Take courage! I AM! Stop being afraid! And Peter answered Him, Lord, if it is You, command me to come to You on the water. He said, Come! So Peter got out of the boat and walked on the water, and he came toward Jesus.

But when he perceived and felt the strong wind, he was frightened, and as he began to sink, he cried out, Lord save me (from death)! Instantly Jesus reached out His hand and caught and held him, saying, O you of little faith, why did you doubt? And when they got into the boat, the wind ceased.

(Matthew 14:24–32)

As long as Peter kept his eyes on Jesus, he was fine, but the moment he began looking down, he became frightened. Doubt and unbelief gripped his heart, and he began sinking. He cried out to Jesus to save him, and He did. I wonder why the storm ceased as soon as Peter got back into the boat! Think about it.

We must keep our eyes on Jesus and not our circumstances. When we rise up we will stop telling God about our problems and begin telling our problems about our God. When the storm comes in your life, dig in and set your face like a flint and be determined to stay out of the boat. Very often the storm ceases as soon as we quit and crawl back into our comfort zone. A ship is safe as long as it's in the harbor; but that not what they are made for.

Rise up and stand tall; do not let the devil intimidate you. During the storm, tell yourself, I can handle this through the power of God for "greater is he that's in you, than he that is in the world."

Doubt Is a Choice

In the early dawn the next morning, as He was coming back to the city, He was hungry. And as He saw one single leafy fig tree above the roadside, He went to it but He found nothing but leaves on it (seeing that in the fig tree the fruit appears at the same time as the leaves). And He said to it, Never again shall fruit grow on you! And the tree withered up at once.

When the disciples saw it, they marveled greatly and asked, How is it that the fig tree has withered away all at once? And Jesus answered them, Truly I say to you, if you have faith (a firm relying trust) and do not doubt, you will not only do what has been done to the fig tree, but even if you say to this mountain, Be taken up and cast into the sea, it will be done.

And whatever you ask for in prayer, having faith and (really) believing you will receive.

(Matthew 21:18–22)

When His disciples marveled and asked Jesus how He was able to destroy the fig tree with just a word, He said to them in essence, "If you have faith and do not doubt you can do the same thing that I have done to the fig tree—and even greater things than this."

(John 14:12)

We already know that faith is a gift from God (Romans 12:3), therefore doubt is a choice. It is the devil's warfare tactic against our minds. Since you can choose your own thoughts, when doubt comes you should learn to recognize it for what it is, say "No, thank you"—rise up, stand tall, and keep on believing.

In concluding there are three questions that sometimes plague the mind: (1) Why is faith so important? (2) How much is necessary for God to work? and (3) Has God changed for this century?

Why is faith so important?

Faith is the criteria by which God works through people.

And the Lord called Samuel again the third time. And he arose and went to Eli, and said, Here am I; for thou didst call me. And Eli perceived that the Lord had called the child. Therefore Eli said unto Samuel, Go, lie down: and it shall be, if he call thee, that thou shalt say, Speak Lord; for thy servant heareth. So Samuel went and lay down in his place.

(1 Samuel 3:8–9)

One would naturally expect an audible message from God to be given to the priest Eli and not to the child Samuel. Eli was older and more experienced, and he held the proper position. But God's chain of command is based on faith. His view of authority and ability is not based on age or position.

When God spoke to Abraham and instructed him to sacrifice his only son Isaac, he arose early the next morning and proceeded to Mount Moriah to give Isaac as a burnt offering. On the third day of the journey, Abraham saw the place in a distance. He instructed his servants to stay with the donkey. Notice what he says in verse 5: "And Abraham said unto his young men, Abide ye here with the ass; and I and the lad will go yonder and worship, and *come again to you*" (emphasis added). Abraham trusted God to the point that he believed if Isaac was slain, God could resurrect him.

We too must have that same kind of faith: "Lord, I don't see it, but I believe it." Even walking through the valleys of life, you must be so confident that your soul can cry out as David: "Yea, though I walk through the valley of the shadow of death, I will fear no evil: for thou are with me; thy rod and thy staff they comfort me" (Psalm 23:4). For we have this assurance: "Surely goodness and mercy shall follow me all the days of my life: and I will dwell in the house of the Lord forever" (Psalm 23:6). God has assured us that He will never leave us nor forsake us; we must believe that and hold on to faith because the day is breaking!

How much faith is necessary for God to work? "And the apostles said unto the Lord, Increase our faith. And the Lord said, If ye had faith as a grain of mustard seed, ye might say unto this sycamine tree, Be thou plucked up by the root" (Luke 17:5–6).

The disciples' question was genuine; they wanted the faith necessary to do what Jesus had been telling them to do. But Jesus didn't directly answer their question because faith is not something we "get." The amount of faith is not as important as its object and its genuineness. Faith is total dependence on God and a willingness to do His will. It is not something we use to put on a show for others. It is complete and humble obedience to God's will, to whatever He ask us to do. The amount of faith isn't as important as the right kind of faith, which is in God.

A mustard seed is small, but it is alive and growing. Like this tiny seed, a small amount of genuine faith in God will take root and grow. Almost invisible at first, it will begin to spread, first underground and then visibly. Although each change will be gradual and imperceptible, soon this faith will have produced major results that will uproot and destroy competing loyalties. We don't need more faith; a tiny seed of faith is enough, if it is alive and growing.

Have God's requirements changed for this century? God doesn't change: "Jesus Christ the same yesterday and today and forever" (Hebrews 13:8). We must keep our eyes on Christ, our ultimate leader, who unlike human leaders, will never change. He has been and will be the same forever. In this changing world, we can trust our unchanging Lord.

Our faith is in the God who created the entire universe by His Word. God's Word has awesome power. When He speaks, things, circumstances, situations, and events change. Many are saying they believe God exists, but believing that God exists is only the beginning; even the demons believe that much (James 2:19–20). God will not settle for your mere acknowledgment of His existence. He wants a personal dynamic, life-transforming relationship with you. Those who sincerely look for this will be rewarded with God's intimate presence.

Noah trusted God and changed the course of history. When he heard God's warning about the future, Noah believed God even though there was no sign of a flood, and wasting no time, he built the ark and saved his family. Noah experienced what it meant to be different from his neighbors. God commanded him to build a huge boat in the middle of dry land, and although God's command seemed foolish, Noah obeyed. Noah's obedience made him appear strange to his neighbors; he stood out.

As you obey God, don't be surprised if others consider you different. Your obedience makes their disobedience stand out. Remember, if God ask you to do something, He will give you the strength to carry out the task. He doesn't change, He still gives strength to the weak, opens the blinded eyes, causes the lame to walk and the dumb to talk. He still heals, saves, and delivers from the beggarly elements of this world. There is nothing out of your reach if you believe God. He said, "Ask and it shall be given you; seek, and ye shall find; knock, and it shall be opened unto you" (Matthew 7:7).

God doesn't change! Do not allow Satan to instill doubt and mistrust in your mind. Stand up and take your rightful place as a child of God. No matter how bad the situation looks, He still stops the lion's mouth, subdues kingdoms, quenches the violence of fires, out of weakness makes you strong, turns to flight the armies of the aliens, brings light out of darkness and peace out of confusion.

Lift up your heads and let the King of Glory come in. If you would lift your hands right where you are now and begin to give God a praise, you will experience that *God doesn't change and the power of God still changes lives through faith*! Remember you are in a fight and only the strong will survive!

What will be your faith response?

When God speaks, what is your faith response? All through Scripture when God revealed Himself, His purpose, and His ways, the response to Him required faith. Faith is confidence that what God has promised or said will come to pass. Sight is an opposite of faith. If you can see clearly how something can be accomplished, more than likely faith is not required. Remember the illustration about our purchasing the land? If we had accepted the fact that we did not have the money to purchase the land, we would have never made that faith move.

Read the following Scriptures and respond to the questions or statements.

1. "Faith is being sure of what we hope for and certain of what we do not see" (Hebrews 11:1). What is faith?

    _____

    _____

    _____

2. "We live by faith, not by sight" (2 Corinthians 5:7). What is an opposite of faith?

    _____

    _____

    _____

3. Jesus said, "Anyone who has faith in me will do what I have been doing. He will do even greater things than these, because I am going to the Father" (John 14:12). What is the potential of faith?

_____

_____

_____

4. "I tell you the truth, if you have faith as small as a mustard seed, you can say to this mountain, 'Move from here to there' and it will move. Nothing will be impossible for you" (Matthew 17:20–21). How much faith is required for God to do through you what is humanly impossible?

_____

_____

_____

5. Paul said, "My message and my preaching were not with wise and persuasive words, but with a demonstration of the Spirit's power, so that your faith might not rest on men's wisdom, but on God's power" (1 Corinthians 2:4–5). On what should we base our faith?

_____

_____

_____

6. On what should we *not* base our faith?

_____

_____

_____

7. "If you do not stand firm in your faith, you will not stand at all" (Isaiah 7:9). What is one danger of lack of faith?

_____

_____

_____

8. Describe a time in your life that required faith, and you did not respond because you lacked faith.

_____

_____

_____

9. Describe a time in your life that required faith in God and you responded in faith. This would be a time when you could see no way to accomplish the task unless God did it through you or in you.

   _____

   _____

   _____

10. What are some hindrances to faith?

    _____

    _____

    _____

11. The average human thinks sixty thousand thoughts per day. How can you change your thought focus to what you desire to create for your life?

    _____

    _____

    _____

12. Fasting has both spiritual and physical benefits; what are they?
    Spiritual: _____
    Physical: _____

13. What are some ways to rid yourself of doubt, fear, and worrying?

    _____

    _____

    _____

14. What is your enemy of faith? How do you plan to deal with it?

    _____

    _____

    _____

15. What do you foresee the power of your faith accomplishing for you in the days ahead?

    _____

    _____

    _____

Epilogue

No matter how steep the mountain—the Lord is going
to climb it with you.

—Helen Steiner Rice

I trust as you read this book your heart was encouraged and your
faith was increased. I am always astonished and amazed when I
read Mark 5:25-34; concerning the woman in the bible with the
issue of blood.

After twelve years, and who knows how many doctors and specialists
and depleted savings, the average person—or faithless person—would
most likely have given up any hope of ever getting better. I'm imagining
depression, frustration, desperation, and despair infiltrating this poor
little woman's mind and plunging her into self-pity and defeat. Why,
the very nature of her illness would indicate physical weakness, loss of
appetite, and perhaps even mental apathy. And just think of going out
in public with her condition. The constant hemorrhaging could have
presented a very embarrassing situation.

However, there was news of a man who was healing all kinds of
diseases and casting out demons: he was even restoring sight to the blind
and speech to some folks that were dumb (faith comes by hearing).
Surely, she must have thought, *If he can do all that, there is hope for even
me. I know that it's going to be quite a challenge to get through the crowds
that are always following him, and all the people who are trying to get his
attention for their needs. But I don't need his attention, or for him to touch
me. All I need is to get close enough to touch his clothes ... or just his hem;
that will be sufficient!*

And so her faith catapulted her into action and into the crowd to get just close enough to Jesus to touch His hem. And the strength of that faith pulled on the Master's virtue and resulted in a miraculous and immediate healing!

Oh, the power of *your* faith can bring results and changes in your life that you wouldn't even expect. When you lend your ear to the Word of God and ignore the negative words of unbelievers and even the voices of reason and logic, the power of your faith can take you beyond logic—above normal, further than ordinary, and past reason—and land you right in the midst of a miracle. You won't even see it coming! You'll know you're there, because your faith can see the evidence way before the results are manifested.

It's the power of your faith!

Notes

Chapter: 1: What Is Faith?

1. *Life Application Study Bible*: New Living Translation, 2nd ed. (Wheaton, Il.: Tyndale House Publishers, Inc., 2004).
2. *Scofield Reference Bible* (New York: Oxford University Press, Inc., new material 1996).
3. Stacy Lawson, "What Is Faith?", www.huffingtonpost.com.
4. *The Life Recovery Bible*: New Living Translation (Wheaton, Illinois: Tyndale House Publishers, Inc., 1998).

Chapter 3: The Power of Thought

1. Chuck Danes, "Enlightened Journey Enterprise," Abundance-and-Happiness.com.
2. *Understanding the Law of Thoughts*, 6th ed. (A Divine Life Society Publication,1997), http://www.shivanandadlshq.org/ (1999).

Chapter 4: What to Do while I'm Waiting

1. Carolyn MacInnes, "In the Meantime: What to Do While Waiting on God." Article, December, 2009, www.boundless.org.

Chapter 6: Doubt: It's a Trap

1. Dale Carnegie, *How to Stop Worrying and Start Living* (New York, New York: Pocket Books, 1985),113.

Chapter 8: Enemies of Faith

1. Kenneth E. Hagin, *The Real Faith* (Tulsa, OK: Kenneth Hagin Ministries,1988).

Chapter 9: How to Keep Faith in Tough Times

1. "Ten Ways to Recharge Your Life," www.beliefnet.com/faith/2008/09/Ten-Ways-to-Recharge-Your-Life.

Chapter 10: Rise Up and Stand Tall!

1. Herbert Lockyear, *All the Doctrines of the Bible* (Zondervan Publishing House, Grand Rapids, Michigan 1964), 193.